CURIOSITIES

—·OF·—

GOLF

CURIOSITIES
OF
GOLF

JONATHAN RICE

CARTOONS BY ROBERT DUNCAN

DEDICATION
For Alex, Liz and Tom, who have cheerfully
put up with my attempts at fatherhood

First published in Great Britain in 1994 by
PAVILION BOOKS LIMITED
26 Upper Ground, London SE1 9PD

Text copyright © Jonathan Rice 1994
Cartoons copyright © Robert Duncan 1994
Title page illustration © Peter Cross 1994

Designed by Nigel Partridge

A CIP catalogue record for this book is available from the
British Library

ISBN 1 85793 281 1

Printed and bound by Butler & Tanner, Frome
Phototypeset in Sabon 10½/17pt by Intype, London

2 4 6 8 10 9 7 5 3 1

This book may be ordered by post direct from the publisher.
Please contact the Marketing Department.
But try your bookshop first.

CONTENTS

INTRODUCTION 7

1 FIRST, COURSES 11

2 HIT ME WITH YOUR RHYTHM STICK 28

3 ROYAL AND ANCIENT 45

4 HEALTHY, WEALTHY AND WISE 65

5 IN BREACH OF THE RULES 83

6 ANIMAL LOVERS 101

7 LIES, DAMNED LIES AND STATISTICS 117

8 THE COURSE OF TRUE LOVE, AND OTHER THINGS . 140

INTRODUCTION

Peter Alliss, the former Ryder Cup golfer who is now a most respected commentator on the game, once noted that 'all games are silly, but golf, if you look at it dispassionately, goes to extremes'. The thing about golf is that nobody ever does look at it dispassionately. From the days over two hundred years ago, when golfers on Blackheath were betting each other a gallon of claret that they could drive 'from the Thorn Tree beyond the College Hole in three strokes, five times in ten', to the 1990s, when there is nothing dispassionate about the prize money available at even the least of the events on the European, Far Eastern and American tours, golf has always been a passion rather than a pastime for those who take part.

Golf is not a safe passion. Keizo Kogure, a Japanese sports doctor, published a book in 1993 entitled *How to Die Early by Playing Golf*, in which he proved that golf is eight times more likely than jogging to kill a man over the age of 60. The golf death rate is higher than for mountaineering, tennis or that most vicious of sports, croquet. Kogure claims that almost 5,000 people a year die on golf courses in Japan. At least this grim epidemic will serve to reduce the queues at each tee at every course in

Japan, where ten million players fight to enjoy themselves on only 2,000 courses. This is the equivalent of 350 people playing on every course every day of the year, assuming only one round per player per fortnight. As the average round takes at least four hours in Japan, it would require a fourball to start every five minutes to enable everybody to get their one round every two weeks. No wonder more Japanese die in the midst of their golfing passion than in the midst of any other kind of passion imaginable.

Not even world wars can put a stop to golf. Richmond Golf Club, in Surrey, established local rules for wartime play, which included the statement that 'a player whose stroke is affected by the simultaneous explosion of a bomb may play another ball from the same place. Penalty one stroke'. At least that proves there are golfers who will admit that the simultaneous explosion of a bomb may put them off their game, if only briefly, but it is of course right that they should not be allowed to use it as an excuse to play again without penalty. Self-control is the secret of success in golf, and any golfer who cannot keep his emotions in check, even when under enemy attack, must inevitably pay the price. And in case you might think that this passion for the game of golf is a peculiarly British stiff upper lip response to crisis, then it should be pointed out that the Japan Open Golf Championship was played annually well beyond Pearl Harbor and the fall of Singapore: in 1942 Tomekichi Miyamoto won the title for the fifth time in nine years. The Germans carried on playing throughout the war, both in their homeland and in occupied Holland and Belgium, and the German Golf Association tried in vain to develop an *ersatz* golf ball when raw materials became scarce.

Because golf is an individual sport, where the true opponent is oneself, curiosities of golf are as frequent and as varied as the curiosities of human nature. And because it is human nature to exaggerate from time to time, there are many reported curiosities which become less curious under the cold glare of reality. What I have tried to do in putting together this book is to eliminate any stories which are clearly unreliable, as well as to avoid as far as possible the really hackneyed tall tales with which everybody who plays golf is not only familiar but fed up to the back teeth. Inevitably, I have included some curiosities which will be well known because they are so curious, but I have also tried to spread my net as wide as possible in coming up with happenings both original and authenticated.

I would like to take this opportunity to thank those people and organizations who have helped in the compilation of this book. I have spent many happy days at the British Newspaper Library at Colindale checking many of the less likely stories, and have also received particular help from Gerald Watts at the Royal St George's GC at Sandwich, who allowed me unmolested access to their library. Others such as Michael Balfour, Sally Bolton, A. Brandie, Geoffrey Coulby, Major L.W. Dickerson, Rachael Heyhoe-Flint, Peter Hughes, Peter Ingram, Gerald Letts, Samantha Mahood, Peter Mason, William J. Morley, Peter Parbery, Chris Pryke, Robin Quantrill, Andy Rice, Liz Rice, John Taylor, Paul Turck, Iain Wallace and Tom Whatson have supplied curiosities which otherwise would have been impossible to turn up. Without their help, this book would have been much shorter.

I should also thank those who have helped in the production of this book. At Pavilion Books, my editor Mandy Greenfield has been a tower of strength. Peter Cross has done his usual extraordinary job with the cover, and Robert Duncan has once again come up with a fantastic clutch of cartoons. Colin Webb deserves the credit for coming up with the idea of curiosities, and for persevering with it. But as usual, any mistakes are my own.

JONATHAN RICE
March 1994

FIRST, COURSES

Macbeth, probably one of the last Scottish kings not to play golf (for the simple reason that it had not yet quite been invented), was nevertheless heard to utter words which have been repeated on countless weekends at countless golf courses in hundreds of countries around the world, as 24 handicappers hack wistfully through another unsuccessful medal round: 'They have tied me to a stake; I cannot fly/ But bear-like I must fight the course.'

All games of golf begin with the course. Most ball games have carefully defined playing areas, with maximum and minimum dimensions and of course the right degree of horizontality to create the 'level playing field' so proudly proclaimed by the politically correct to be the basis of all that is fair in British life. It is therefore a perverse twist of fate that the true thrill of the most successfully exported ball game of all those invented by the British in their idle hours lies not so much in man being pitted against man as in man being pitted against the very ground he walks on. The real competition is against the twisted mind that designed the course in the first place, not against the poor sap who like you is desperately trying to hack his way through sand, heather, gorse and the occasional river in something under a hundred. We must all, like Macbeth, fight the course, and it gives us no comfort to remember that within 61 lines of his baleful cry, Macbeth has exited, fighting. A mere 21 lines later, his head re-enters stage left, along with Macduff, but the rest of his body remains elsewhere. The course has won again.

The first golf courses were not laid out by man but by God. They were wild areas by the sea shore, too poor to be agriculturally viable and often too windswept to graze sheep on. One can almost imagine the glint in the Creator's eye as he shaped the terrain on the east coast of Scotland and then gave Man the gift of free will to invent golf to go with it. Golf is not meant to be an easy game. Many would maintain that fairways are not meant to be particularly well groomed, that the rough should indeed be rough, and that hazards and traps should be there for the wary as well as the unwary. Not for the true golfer the rather feeble attitude displayed by an article in *Golf Illustrated*

in March 1936. The article was headed, 'Water Hazards – Are They Justified on a Golf Course?' and the conclusion was that 'the use of water is often overdone'.

The secretary of Gorleston Golf Club in Norfolk would probably agree. In 1960 it was reported that a Miss L. Holmsen and her father, Mr T.W. Holmsen, were taking their regular walk along a fjord in Norway, when Miss Holmsen noticed a large piece of wood floating in the water. On closer inspection, it was seen to state, 'Gorleston Golf Club – PRIVATE'. The Holmsens may not have known very much about golf, but they would have been aware that unless some of the Gorleston members had been on a raid to avenge the suffering of their East Anglian ancestors at the hands of the Vikings, this notice must have gone astray. Miss Holmsen wrote to the club, who told her that the signboard had been lost from the cliffs near the links the previous summer. In grateful thanks for having their sign returned, the club granted honorary membership to the Holmsens, but it is not recorded whether they ever actually played the course. It would be a daunting prospect to play at a club where one of the water hazards is the North Sea.

A rather smaller hazard is the River Siagne, which runs through the course at Golf de Cannes Mandelieu. The course, originally created by Archduke Michael of Russia, the brother of Tsar Nicholas II, was often used by the Duke of Windsor and by King Leopold of Belgium, probably the best royal golfer of all. But even royalty cannot walk on the water. Ferries are installed at various points to take golfers from green to tee. When Littlehampton Golf Club

13

in West Sussex was opened in 1889, a ferry was used to cross the River Arun, as the only road crossing was upstream at Arundel. A swing bridge was opened in 1908, but the ferry was still in operation until well after the Second World War. Nowadays, rather boringly, the river plays no part in the average golfer's round. It would require a very wild shot to hit the river.

Golf balls used to be made to float (the Slazenger 'Boodie' golf ball of 1899 was just one example of a ball 'warranted to float'), but since the gutta-percha ball was superseded by the denser rubber-cored ball, the floating ball is no longer with us. This is a major disappointment to those of us who would gladly give up yardage off the tee to feel more secure in the knowledge that our balls would not disappear for ever if by some unlikely fluke we sliced the damn thing into the nearest patch of water. But the floating ball may have created the longest golf hit ever recorded. One Thomas O. Hampson wrote to *Golf Illustrated* in June 1935, stating that he had recently been surveying in Northern Labrador, at a place called Nukusu-sutok, a few miles seaward of the village of Nain. 'On the slope of a hill and about 300 feet inland,' wrote Mr Hampson, 'I found a golf ball in good condition. How did the ball come to be there, and so far inland? It is possible that the ball was driven by a golfer from an Atlantic liner during practice, drifted northward past Greenland and was finally carried ashore by the Labrador current.' No other solution to the enigma of the Labrador golf ball was ever offered, but a drive from an Atlantic liner, past Greenland and on to Nukususutok, could be as far as 1,500 miles, a shot of which even John Daly would be proud.

15

Would golf be the challenge we all know it to be if there was not the ancient element of water to contend with, as well as the other elements of earth, air and fire? The element of fire is not always present on a golf course, but it is as well to be prepared. Many courses, especially in southern Europe and the western United States, have been ravaged by fires, something which is comparatively rare in the muggier climate of the British Isles. All the same, in 1976, fire devastated two courses in Dorset, Broadstone and Ferndown. At Ferndown, a forest bordering the 15th hole was completely destroyed by fire and fire swept across the 15th fairway, and then jumped across the 16th fairway, before stopping up against the boundary fence. The fire had broken out on ladies' medal day, and firemen were a little surprised to see two members emerge from the smoke wearing handkerchieves over their faces as smoke masks. They said they could not see why a little fire should stop them finishing their round. It is not known whether either of these intrepid ladies won the medal that day, but they deserved to. In 1927, it was reported that a golfer in South Africa tried to play through a small bush fire, but lost not only his ball, scorched when he hit into the blazing semi-rough, but also his clubs when his golf bag caught fire. The problem with hickory shafts is that they burn rather more easily than graphite or steel.

The element of air is always a problem. Once the wind starts to blow, golf becomes a different game. Everybody knows that, so it is not a curiosity. In 1938, a hurricane disrupted the final day of the Open at Sandwich. The exhibition tent was totally destroyed and its contents were scattered over the landscape. Thirty-six holes were played that day, and only Reg Whitcombe, the eventual winner, Henry Cotton and James Adams broke 80 in both rounds. In 1960, a period of strange golfing weather around the globe, gale force winds blew several cars on to the fairways of the Monterey Peninsula Country Club in California, one landing only a few feet from a large sign reading 'Autos Keep Off Fairways – Orders Of The Green

Committee'. What sort of a golf course is it that has to remind its members not to drive cars on the fairways?

But the main problem with any course is the element of earth. Most golf courses consist of grasses of many and varied types, trees and bushes, earth, sand and water. By the end of each round, it is usually possible for the typical high-handicapper to describe from first-hand experience most of the different textures of grass that make up the rough and the semi-rough, to give chapter and verse about any thicket of trees alongside the fairways, and to evoke a clear word picture of the depth and consistency of the sand in many of the bunkers. Generally, however, he or she will tell you that the grass was green and the sand was – well, sandy coloured. It is unusual for them to mention that the greens were blue. But at Bulawayo in what was then Southern Rhodesia, in the 1930s, the greens were laid with a 'diamondiferous gravel', which gave them a very pronounced blue tint. In March 1943, a disgruntled golfer wrote to an American golfing magazine, saying that 'the course at Dodoma, Tanganyika Territory, is well up in the running for distinction as the world's worst course. The surface of the entire course is a hard substance similar to asphalt.' Dodoma's main challenger is probably one of the courses in Kuwait, where, just after the Gulf War, there were slit trenches on the fairways, and mines in the rough. One course, it is said, lost six holes 'due to the emplacement of Patriot missile batteries'. That must have been quite a committee meeting which gave the go-ahead to that.

At the other end of the scale come courses like

17

Charnwood Forest, in Leicestershire, a 4,960 yard par-69 course which has no bunkers. Playing 18 holes without once having to pull out the sand wedge might sound like perfection to many of us, but experience shows that it does not necessarily improve one's game. In 1898 a five-man team of Charnwood Forest golfers went to play a match against Notts Forest at the Bulwell Forest course in Nottingham, where there are bunkers as well as the usual water hazards and patches of impenetrable rough. They lost by a quite spectacular margin. In 180 holes of golf, the Charnwood Forest five went down by a combined total of 43 holes, with only their third string, G.P. Brand, lasting to the inward half of the final round. How many times they tried to fight their way out of the unfamiliar sand is not recorded, but *The Golfer* magazine merely mentions that 'the losers must have quitted Bulwell thinking that the Corporation should have had the ground for a cemetery as they had wanted.' It was certainly a burial ground for their golf that day.

Golf without sand is to many like an egg without salt – too bland for anything other than relieving the appetite. At Golf de St Malo Le Tronchet, in northern France, they have taken matters to the other extreme, and the bunker which runs alongside the 18th hole is reputedly the largest in Europe. It is also quite possibly the oldest in Europe, for hidden iceberg-like within this bunker (and in the one that straddles the 16th hole) are ancient Druidic stones, of great archaeological importance and little golfing use. Even this enormous bunker, however, must pale beside the one alongside the 17th hole at Pine Valley Golf Club in

New Jersey, which is an acre and a half in area. The 1936 Walker Cup was played there, and the British team failed to win a single match, managing only to halve one of the singles and two of the foursomes.

Golf in the sand is becoming more and more a part of the golfing year, with European Tour events played in Dubai, Agadir and at other desert courses. The Emirates Golf Course in Dubai came about because Sheikh Moham-med bin Rashid al Maktoum was intrigued by the fact that television coverage of his beloved horse racing was continually being interrupted by visits to a golf tourna-ment. The Sheikh decided that this curious game merited further investigation. He brought in the American golf course architect Karl Litten to design an all-grass course for the desert. When asked how much he thought it would cost, Litten was unsure how much he should quote, or even what currency he should quote in. Playing safe, he just said, 'Three to five million'. The Sheikh looked a little surprised, and replied, '325 million dollars seems rather a lot.' The final cost was somewhere in between the two figures.

An all-grass course in the desert is better than an all-desert course in the desert, but golfers in South Australia have little option. The Eldo Desert Classic is played at the Woomera course four hundred miles north of Adelaide. The course, where golfers have to watch out for copper-head snakes, is generously described as 'very sandy'. In fact, there is no grass at all, and the club motto is 'Eat My Dust'. At the nearby Roxby Downs course, at least six of the eighteen greens have grass on them, but as it is the site of a huge uranium mine, golfers do not flock to play there, unless they have a particular desire to glow in the dark.

Sand is a trap for even the greatest golfers, and so is the rough. 'That the rough be cut immediately after the Championship' is a suggestion dated 17 May 1959 in the Royal St George's GC suggestion book, signed by four members. 'Don't agree with above' is another member's response. 'It makes good golfers casual and bad golfers conceited.' Two more members have added their signatures to this view, after one of which is written, 'A noble sentiment after losing eleven balls.' The rough at Sandwich is really rough. However, the suggestion dated 16 October 1937 – 'that the Club provide an anti-aircraft gun near the ninth green' – was not because the rough was too short to camouflage ground troops. War was looming. 'Would suggest that General Maginot be asked for plans of a portable concrete fort, fully equipped with Bollinger '21, Cockburn '08 and Kummel', reads another suggestion that year by a member who would need comfort in his search for lost balls in the rough, war or no war.

In July 1932, *American Golfer* magazine reported the existence of what was then considered to be the most northerly course in the world. At Chesterfield Inlet on Hudson Bay, the Tundra Golf Club had a membership of just four people: Revd William Marsh, an Anglican missionary; Father Ducharme, a Catholic missionary; T.C. Carmichael, the Hudson's Bay Company factor; and Bob Fowler, Mr Carmichael's assistant. In true imperialist style, the Eskimos caddied for them. Only three holes had been finished in 1932, as it was a very hard job building a golf

course on the frozen land. Grass would not grow, of course, so the greens were made of hard packed sand.

Grass did not grow at the Piltdown Golf Club in Sussex in 1960, either. Somebody scattered sodium chlorate over the greens, which did them no good at all. Sea water is what they needed. When Felixstowe Ferry GC's course was flooded by the sea in the storms of October 1897, the club feared that it would be years before they would be able to play the full course again. But by February the next year, the captain was able to state that the salt water had helped the course wonderfully. 'I have never seen the course looking better,' he added. All the same, a sea wall was built.

Some people dispense with golf courses altogether. Cross-country golf was once a great craze, although in these days of motorways and electrified railway lines, it is not as common as it used to be. In Ireland, there was the 'Golden Ball' competition, which involved teeing off at the first tee at Cill Dara, and holing out at the 18th at the Curragh, about 8,800 yards (5 miles) away. A prize of £1 million was offered for a hole in one, which has yet to be claimed. The first 'Golden Ball' competition was won by the great Irish amateur, Joe Carr, in 52 strokes.

Carr's victory, at an average of about 170 yards per shot, was a remarkable achievement. Cross-country golfers tend to average rather less mileage per hit than that. Most golf courses will require an average shot length of about 90 yards (6,500 yards, par-72, for example), and although cross-country golfers do not have to worry about 6-foot putts, they have less fairway than on the average course, so any cross-country golfer who averages much more than 100 yards per stroke is either a very good golfer or else a very good liar.

In 1920, Rupert Lewis (or possibly Phillips – different authorities disagree) and W. Raymond Thomas played over 20 miles from Radyr Golf Club near Cardiff to South-erndown Golf Club at Ewenny, near Bridgend. One of the conditions was that the rules of golf were to be strictly observed. There were many bets on the outcome, most punters feeling that at least 1,000 strokes would be needed. Playing alternate strokes, they completed the route in a mere 608 strokes (just under 60 yards per shot), in 16 hours, including intervals for refreshment. At one time, the pair had to wade knee deep to ford a river, but dried out by jumping a hedge while being chased by a bull. Twenty balls were lost (most of them in the river, no doubt) and, as *Golf Illustrated* reports, 'the proper penalty was paid'.

In June 1986, eight members of Barnet Rugby Hackers Golf Club, described somewhat inadequately by *The Times*

22

as 'a group of rotten golfers', played a game of golf from
Prestwick, the site of the first Open Championship, to
Turnberry, where that year's event was taking place. The
route took them even farther than Messrs Thomas and
Phillips (or Lewis), for some 23 miles across Ayrshire,
beginning on the afternoon of Monday 23 June and finishing just after lunch the next day. They lost only 50 or 60
balls, in completing the course, which had been inspired
by a P.G. Wodehouse short story, 'The Long Hole', in
which Arthur Jakes and Ralph Bingham played a cross-
country golf match for the hand of one Amanda Trivett.
No such prize was at stake as the Barnet Hackers hooked
and sliced their way across the Scottish countryside, which
was perhaps fortunate as, in the Wodehouse story, Miss
Trivett gets engaged to somebody else altogether. Of
course, in real life it rained, but on their way to the finish
at Turnberry's 18th hole, followed very quickly by
Turnberry's 19th hole, the eight Hackers negotiated a holiday camp, a dockyard, a stately home, a croquet lawn,
several roofs, the River Doon and a large bull. In Wodehouse's story, the main obstacles were a car door and a
casual dog, which accounts for the scores of 1,100 shots
which had been recorded by the time they had covered
but 16 miles and were in sight of their goal. For the record,
Hackers captain John Taylor's team of four claimed victory
over rival John Bee's team by the widely reported but
almost certainly underestimated total of 375 shots to 385.
Approximately.

Belting a ball across Ayrshire is not the most difficult or
uncomfortable way of playing the game. The Aberdeen-

23

born WPGA professional Muriel Thomson flew out to the BP Forties Field Charlie platform in the spring of 1981 to give golf clinics to the oilmen. As Muriel flew in by helicopter, the platform was being lashed by 60-knot winds and 20-foot waves, which made landing very difficult and teeing up completely impossible.

Capt. Alan Shepard remains the only man to have played golf on the moon. The Apollo 14 astronaut drove two balls on 7 February 1971, using a special 6-iron head attached to the handle of his contingency sample return device. The bulk of his spacesuit meant that he had to hit one-handed, and his claimed distance of 200 yards for the first shot is perhaps a little over-optimistic. *The Guinness Book of Records* claimed that 'on the moon, the energy expended on a mundane 300-yard drive would achieve, craters permitting, a distance of a mile', but Capt. Shepard achieved nowhere near that distance. Perhaps that is because he, like many others, would not consider a 300-yard drive 'mundane'. All the same, these were the golf shots that were seen by more people than any other shots in the history of golf, on a course that only two people, Capt. Shepard and his fellow astronaut Edgar Mitchell, have ever visited.

DROPPED SHOTS

Drive off in England and hole out in Wales
345-yard 4th hole at Llanmynech Golf Club, Oswestry

Driving range where balls are hit into a lake,
Kissimmee Bay GC, Florida

Golf on the equator
Nanyuki, Kenya (6,500 feet up). The town is in the Southern hemisphere, the course in the Northern hemisphere

Golf 150 miles within the Arctic Circle
Bjorkliden Arctic Golfklubb, Sweden

Golf at 22,834 feet above sea level
Gerald Williams, from the summit of Mount Aconcagua, Argentina, 22 January 1989

Golf at 20,320 feet above sea level
Timothy Ayers, from the summit of Mount McKinley, Alaska, USA, 23 May 1984

Golf courses over 8,000 feet above sea level include
Tuctu Golf Club, Morococha, Peru, 14,335 feet
La Paz Golf Club, Bolivia, 13,500 feet
Indian Army golf course, Indo-Tibetan border (incomplete), 12,800 feet
Oruro Golf Club, Bolivia, 11,000 feet
Cloudcroft Golf Club, New Mexico, 9,000 feet
Gulmarg Golf Club, Kashmir, India, 8,500 feet
Arequipa Golf Club, Peru, 8,367 feet

Golf at 6,500 feet above sea level
Golf Sestrieres, Italy

Golf in Scotland at 1,500 feet above sea level
Leadhills Golf Club, Strathclyde

Golf in Wales at 1,300 feet above sea level
Tredegar Park Golf Club, Gwent

Golf in England at 1,250 feet above sea level
Church Stretton Golf Club, Shropshire

Golf at 1,250 feet below sea level
Sodom and Gomorrah Golf Club, Kallia, Israel (club house burnt down in 1948)

Golf club with only two members
Golf International les Bordes, France

Golf course which becomes a ski resort in the winter
Golf de Mont d'Arbois, Megève, France

Funicular railway required to reach the 11th tee
Golf de Sainte-Maxime, near St Tropez, France

Sky gondola required to reach first tee from car park
Waterway Hills GC, South Carolina, USA

Golf courses encircled by horse race track
Ludlow Golf Club, Shropshire; Kelso Golf Club, Roxburghshire; Uttoxeter, Staffordshire; Golf de Compiègne, France; Golf Club Stadtwald, Krefeld, Germany

Golf course which used to be a horse race track
Honourable Company of Edinburgh Golfers GC, Muirfield

Course cut in two by motorway
Estoril Palacio GC, Portugal

18-hole course with only 12 greens
Golf Club du Château Royal d'Ardenne, Belgium

From Tower Bridge to White's Club in 142 shots using a putter
Richard Sutton, 23 April 1939

Through central Pittsburgh, Pa. (5 miles) in 199 shots
William Patton, 1899

From Linton Park, Maidstone to Littlestone (26 miles) in 1,087 shots
T.H. and A.G. Oyler, April 1898

From Mobile GC, Alabama, to San Antonio GC, Texas (850 miles) in 30,930 shots and with 105 lost balls
Doe Grahame, 1927

Across the United States from west to east (3,398 miles) in 114,737 strokes and with 3,511 lost balls
Floyd Satterlee Rood, 14 September 1963 to 3 October 1964

HIT ME WITH YOUR RHYTHM STICK 2

Finding a golf course to play on is not too difficult; after all there are over 3,000 of the things in Europe alone. Finding the best of all possible equipment with which to play the very best of all possible golf is quite a different matter. There is so much to learn and so many mistakes to be made. In 1898, a report in *The Golfer* told of a player on a public seaside course not far from Edinburgh. He had a full set of clubs, all left-handed, but to the astonishment of onlookers, he addressed the ball on the first tee in a right-handed style. 'He succeeded in wading round the links playing always in the same way, hitting the ball with the back of his clubs. When asked how he got on, he replied, "Very well, seeing it was my first game".'

Another man playing his first round of golf had a more basic problem. In the middle of the last century, Viscount Stormont, who was then over sixty years old and by all accounts much too fat, was told by his doctor to 'go down to Blackheath and put yourself in the hands of Willie Dunn', who was the custodian there. Lord Stormont bought a full set of clubs, and set out to play as the doctor had ordered. After five holes, his caddie Weever was sent

back to the professional's shop with all the club heads in his pocket, and bits of the shafts under his arm, with instructions to bring a new set. At the end of the day, Willie Dunn sympathized with Lord Stormont. 'Don't mention it,' said the noble lord. 'I feel that already this game has done me a great deal of good, and it is going to do me still more.' He then outlined his future plans. 'I shall be down again on Thursday, and please have another set of clubs ready for me then.'

Ah, but the eternal question then arises – which clubs are best for me? Over the years a massive range of clubs have been invented, patented, tested and in some cases even manufactured and used on the golf course, although the number that go successfully through all stages of this process from mind to matter are far fewer than their inventors would wish. How does a golfer decide which clubs to use? Should one try the whistling golf club, patented by Mr L. Challenor of Cheadle Hulme in 1936? The club had several holes in the club head, on the theory that 'air, entering and passing through the holes during the making of the stroke, will tend to keep the club straight, or straighten any tendency to leave the direct line, so that the moment it reaches the ball it will be in the position it was placed when addressing the ball', which is fine if you addressed the ball correctly in the first place, but less helpful to those of us who cannot even get that part right. 'A further instructive feature is that the passage of air through the holes will produce a distinctive sound, which may assist the player to correct an error in the stroke.' The sound may have been distinctive, but I doubt if it was very musical. The man with the whistling clubs would not, I feel, have been the most popular partner for a quiet midweek evening round. If one is concerned to achieve maximum impact with the ball on all occasions, perhaps the keen golfer should acquire the Craig Golfmeter, which cost a mere $27.50 when first advertised in 1923. The Craig Golfmeter, which looked rather like a foghorn with a ball attached to a piece of string dangling from the end, was supposed to 'correct any fault, stance, swing lifting the head or swinging the body'. Rather cryptically, the advertisement added the information that 'Babcock chart attachments add interest to Golfmeter play'. But then, Babcock chart attachments add interest to anything.

How many clubs does one need to play championship golf? The regulation these days is no more than 14 clubs, but Harry Vardon used only nine clubs while Lawson Little, who won the British Amateur title twice in the 1930s, and on turning professional won the US Open in 1940, carried 24 clubs in his bag. This vast total was more connected with sponsorship than the demands of the course. Capt. G.M.F. Molesworth, who won the Dowie Silver Cup at Hoylake in 1870 and who was a pillar of the Westward Ho! GC, only possessed three clubs: a 'play club' which he called Faith, an iron called Hope and a putter called Charity. The putter was Captain Molesworth's key weapon, for as St Paul's epistle to the Corinthians teaches us, 'the greatest of these is Charity'. A more modern golfing and religious expert puts it equally succinctly. 'Drive for show, putt for dough.' Unfortunately, the good Captain found it very difficult to get the ball into the air with any of his clubs, and thus earned the nickname of 'The Mole'.

In 1955, a competitor was disqualified from the Amateur Championship for having one too many clubs in his bag. He had been practising his driving before his round, and had stayed too long on the practice ground. He rushed to the first tee, stuffing his driver in his bag as he went, and played the first hole, a short one, with an iron. It was not until the second hole that he realized that he had 15 clubs in his bag, and at that time disqualification was the automatic penalty. These days he would just have lost the first hole.

There have been more variations on the putter than on any other club in the history of golf. Sam Torrance is one of the pioneers of the 'broomhandle' putter, which looks odd but seems to work for him, as it did for the first three in the 1993 Australian Masters. Winner Bradley Hughes, runner-up Peter Senior (who lost in the play-off, largely because he was put off by a photographer's flash gun on the final green), and third placed Terry Price all used the broomhandle putter to devastating effect. But before the broomhandle there were many other weird and wonderful

designs. In 1904, Walter Travis became the first American to win the British Amateur Championship, but he did so using the revolutionary Schenectady putter (a croquet mallet style putter) which was subsequently made illegal. The Triangular Adjustable putter, marketed by the Baltimore Putter Co. in the 1920s at a price of $8.00, was based on the rather flimsy theory that 'golfers want a putter that gives them three lofts for right-hand and three lofts for left-hand players'. This sounds more like a clubhouse than a putter. All adjustable golf clubs, even those with lofts and a granny annexe, were soon banned.

The most unpleasant idea for a golf club must surely be that of the American company, Sportsman's Memorials Inc. Their unique selling point is to place the cremated remains of your nearest and dearest in the shaft of his or her favourite golf club. For a mere $100 or so, they will decant your ashes into the handle of any club you nominate. It would be a significant test of character to decide whether one would prefer to spend eternity suffering major G forces inside the handle of the driver you used so often and so unsuccessfully, or whether to pass the years rustling around in the putter that let you down consistently whenever there was anything at stake.

Making golf clubs is really more of an alchemist's than an undertaker's art. The great clubmakers, from Hugh Philp and Robert Forgan to Ben Sayers and Karsten Solheim, have had a messianic zeal in the way they have created their beautiful implements. And of course it is a profitable art, rather more profitable than attempting the alchemist's better publicized trick of turning base metal into gold. A Philp club will sell at auction these days for sums well into five figures, and Karsten Solheim, the inventor of the Ping range of clubs, was estimated in 1993 to be worth $450 million, which is a lot more than the professionals using his clubs have earned. It is the equivalent of winning every prize, from first place down to the very bottom of the barrel, in every PGA professional event for 16 seasons from 1977. As the Ping phenomenon only really got started when Julius Boros won the Phoenix Open in 1967 using a Ping putter, it has taken Mr Solheim barely a quarter of a century to amass greater wealth than any handful of top professionals of the same era combined. So many others have tried to develop clubs as good as Mr Solheim's. Now we have the Plop putter, as used by Seve Ballesteros in the 1993 Ryder Cup (not necessarily a good advertisement, that), which is customized by means of computerized sensors to ensure a comfortable putting position. Then there is the Ball Rholer, designed to eliminate skidding. 'Weights can be added or removed to cater for the speed of the greens without changing your stroke.'

33

And there are a hundred others, all with the secret of perfect putting locked up inside them. As industrialists have known for many years, it is far more profitable to manufacture the weapons of war than to use them.

Not that Solheim would have made much money out of Sam Snead, the great American professional, if he had been manufacturing clubs in Snead's heyday. Snead used the same driver throughout his career. But the manufacturers of golf balls need never worry that a player will use the same one throughout his career. For most of us it is an achievement to use the same ball throughout one hole, let alone one career. In 1993, it was calculated that Britain's 1,250,000 golfers lose 32.3 million golf balls a year, or about 26 balls per player per year. American golfers are far more accurate. They are reported to lose only 96 million balls every year, which is a mere four balls per player per year. This compares with the light-hearted article in *Golf Illustrated* in May 1916 which recorded the fact that '$500,000 worth of golf balls are lost each Saturday. There are also found golf balls to the value of $345.75. The energy expended by these golfers would beat 100,000 carpets, thus throwing 5,000 men permanently out of work.' These days the carpet-beating industry does not employ quite so many people, but the point is well taken. How many people would be thrown out of work if somebody invented the unlosable golf ball?

There have been many attempts to create this perfect product. It all began in the sixteenth century when James VI of Scotland (soon to become James I of England) appointed one James Melvile 'golf ball maker for Scotland', and gave him a monopoly for 21 years. He also ruled that any golf balls not stamped with Melvile's name would be confiscated: this was an early attempt to prevent cheap imports from swamping the market. Three hundred years later, Melvile's monopoly had been ended long enough for W.T. Henley's Telegraph Works Co. Ltd., of London to advertise in January 1898 their new 'Melfort' ball. 'Has an excellent flight, paint will not chip and it floats,' ran the copy. That covers most of the average golfer's difficulties, but Alex Clark and Son of Montrose had a supplementary answer to help even further. 'Old Friends With New Faces', proclaimed their advertisement. 'Clean And Paint Your Golf Balls Now! – The Best Paint, White Or Red, 9d, post free.' Alexander Henry, a rifle maker in Edinburgh, was obviously not making enough profit out of the Boer War, so in 1899 he began advertising Henry's Patent Rifled Ball (protected under patent 4630, 22 February 1898). Unfortunately he did not explain how it worked.

35

In the 1950s, Professor O.S. Sinnatt MC, DSC, FRAeS invented a gyroscopic golf ball which would neither slice nor pull. He offered the project to the North British Rubber Company, but they did not go ahead with manufacturing and marketing the idea because they felt it would not be in the best interests of golf. Also, the length of a drive with the gyroscopic ball was less than with a regulation ball because part of the forward energy of the ball is used to produce rotational energy by the exertion of the gyroscopic torque necessary to keep the sliced ball on a direct path. In other words, if your drive is a natural slice, the ball won't go very far, which seems to me exactly what is needed. There is nothing more frustrating than seeing your slices disappear out of bounds 250 yards away, when if only they had stopped after 60 yards or so, you would at least not be three on the tee.

If you don't want to paint your golf balls, if you can't find one that floats and if you still slice the damn thing into the wildest part of the course, then maybe you need the new Trakflite ball. Developed by Mr William Barnhill, the Trakflite has a small battery, electric circuitry and a bleeper in its core. When struck by a golf club, the Trakflite emits a shrill shriek that can be heard up to 100 yards away. I have heard people when they lose their golf balls emitting a shriek that can be heard up to 100 yards away, but not even the worst golfers I know do this every time they hit the ball. Mr Barnhill's invention could do for social golf what the Sex Pistols did for the lullaby.

Just as you are beginning to fear that a quiet few holes are to be a thing of the past, Dr Eric Farr, a Scottish

scientist, has come up with a ball that is both quiet and unlosable. This is because it is square, or to be more precise, a cube. The idea is that you use this ball not out on the 434-yard par-5 16th, but during quiet moments in the home or the office. The square ball is made of hollow rubber, which can be filled with sand or water to restrict the distance it moves. After years of dealing with sand and water filled with golf balls, we now have golf balls filled with sand and water. Much more to the taste of most golfers is the ball filled with brandy, marketed by Grants Morella Cherry Brandy to commemorate the 1993 Open at Sandwich.

If you do lose your golf balls, there is hope, especially if you are in New Zealand or Ascot. In 1971 Chico the dog was made an honorary member of Waihi GC, near Hamilton on the North Island of New Zealand. He had what was described as 'an infallible nose for finding golf balls', and in the first few months of 1971, he had already found enough balls to raise NZ$30 for club funds by selling them back to club members. I feel that this would not have made Chico the most popular member of the club, except among committee men. When playing in Bermuda, I hit three consecutive drives into a small lake, from which they were immediately fished by local youths, who sold them back to me in time for me to hit them straight back into the water. By the end of this little panto-mime, I did not harbour particularly warm feelings towards these lads, however useful they felt their contri-bution to the local economy was. Golfers tend not to like having their shortcomings pointed out quite so clearly.

At Mill Ride Golf Club, Ascot, the sub-aqua team of the 1st Battalion, the Parachute Regiment, were dropped by helicopter on 12 December 1993 into a lake by the 3rd hole, where more than 10,000 golf balls were thought to have landed over the years. Throughout the day, in temperatures barely above freezing, the team fished thousands of balls out of the lake, which were taken away to be cleaned and sold to raise funds for the NSPCC and the Airborne Forces Security Fund. A second dive in the spring of 1994 brought the total of balls recovered from the lake to well over the original estimate, and raised several thousand pounds for the nominated charities. The golf pro at Mill Ride clearly has much to teach the members about length and direction at the 3rd hole.

The important thing with a golf ball is to note carefully the make and number; so that there can be no confusion about it. Duffy Waldorf, the American professional, uses balls marked by his wife Vicky and his son Tyler, which are so colourful that there is never any doubt whose ball it is. One of the balls he used in the Open at Sandwich in 1993 bore the legend, 'Hit Me Further', which Duffy did well enough to finish joint 39th. Other top golfers are superstitious about the numbers on their balls. Payne Stewart likes high numbers, but most other professionals like a low number, which will with any luck match their score. Yet Severiano Ballesteros says the number 3 is unlucky, and Eamonn Darcy and Darren Clarke, among others, will never use a 1 ball.

A ball which nobody ever really liked to use, and which has now disappeared from pro shop shelves all over the

world is the type invented by Mr W. Langstaff in 1912. His patent, no. 16488, was for a new type of golf ball. None of this gutta percha, feathers or rubber for Mr Langstaff. His patent specified that 'the core of the golf ball shall consist of a bull's penis, first prepared by skimming and drying'.

The practice golf ball, that plastic thing with holes in it, is not usually used for anything other than honing the swing in the back garden. However, at the Addington course, at Croydon, Surrey in the 1950s, a bet was made between two members that a round could not be completed with a quarter-ounce plastic ball in fewer than 750 strokes. The winner of the bet, which was for 1,000 guineas (£1,050), managed to complete the 18 holes in 409 strokes. His best hole was a 13 and his worst a 57.

In January 1899, Andrew Spence even wrote a song about his golf ball. He called it 'The Gutta Ba', and its opening couplet was, 'O give me a game at gowf, boys/To drive away the blues.' The astonishing thing about this song is that it was written fifteen years before the first hit recording of a blues song in America, 'Memphis Blues', in 1914. That song was written by W.C. Handy, who wrote his immortal 'St Louis Blues' the same year. Before then, the word 'blues' had rarely been used in song. Perhaps, after all, the blues originated in St Andrews rather than the Mississippi delta.

Golf clubs and golf balls are not the only items needed to complete a round of golf. You need a glove or, in Ian Woosnam's case, at least half a dozen. He once got through five gloves in one intensive afternoon of practice. It is a curiosity that over 60 per cent of male professional golfers, including the 'Golden Bear', Jack Nicklaus, have such small hands that they insist on an 'S' fitting glove. Eamonn Darcy is one of the few who need an 'XL' fitting, but at the other end of the scale José Maria Olazabal has to have special extra small gloves made for him. His hands are even smaller than those of any of the professionals on the women's circuit.

As well as gloves, you need all the right clothes. As P.G. Wodehouse so rightly observed in his classic story, *The Magic Plus Fours*, 'it was the costume that did it. It was not because they were crack players that crack players wore Plus Fours: it was because they wore Plus Fours that they were crack players.' To kit out the European Ryder Cup team in 1993, even without magic plus-fours, the cost was conservatively estimated at £50,000. For the six days of the event (three practice days and three days when the golf was for real) each player was provided with two pairs of Oscar Jacobson golf trousers per day, two Glenmuir polo tops and two sweaters, one sleeveless and one long-sleeved. Then they were given a complete set of Pro-Quip rain gear, two pairs of Foot-Joy shoes and many gloves. The package also included off-course wear by Hugo Boss (a suit, a blazer, two pairs of trousers and six shirts each). The cost of chewing gum, Polo mints and tonic drinks would have to be added. After the Ryder Cup, much of the clothing is auctioned for charity, because any player who is contracted to another manufacturer for his professional life outside the Ryder Cup will not be able to wear the Ryder Cup kit in any other tournament.

41

Looking right is a crucial part of success at golf. The dress code at Burntisland in Fife at the turn of the century was strict. 'The Burntisland Ladies have decided,' wrote Horatio Hutchinson in March 1899, 'by a majority, to don a red jacket with black passementerie, and hats trimmed with red. We ought all to be thankful that a proposal for a rational costume was vetoed.' The Blackheath golfers set the trend for playing in red coats. The rules of the Blackheath Club as set out in 1844 include the statement that 'members shall appear in their Red Coats on the Medal Days', a rule that was not dropped for a further 45 years.

The idea of wearing a rational costume for golf is taking a long while to be adopted, if Payne Stewart's outfits are anything to go by. Always clad in plus-fours, he wears the colours of different American Football teams on different days of tournaments, and thus clashes not only with his playing partners and the gallery, but also with the natural colours of the courses on which he plays. This does not seem to prevent him from playing consistently well.

Whether the Patent 1279 Windsor Trouser Breeches, advertised as exactly what the discerning golfer should be wearing, helped their owners to play consistently well, is not recorded, probably because one of the main advantages of the Trouser Breeches was that 'Jack Boots may be comfortably worn'. It has never been advisable to criticize anybody wearing jack boots, however bad their golf.

An often overlooked part of the golfer's essential equipment is the tee. In 1899, a Scottish golfer was reported to have invented a nail tee. The editor of *Golfer's Magazine* reported that he had 'not yet had experience of one so I cannot say; but if a foozled drive sends a two-inch nail through the air, I would rather not be in the vicinity. We are not all like Mr Jeffrey of the Derby Club, who with his iron lifted a ball off very thin ice covering a pond, and did not crack the ice.' Harold Gillies, at the 1924 Amateur Championship at St Andrews, was one of a handful of golfers who used freak tees which set the ball a foot above the ground. He then hit the ball with an abnormally deep-faced club. There is nothing in the rules to limit the height at which a ball can be teed, and thus to prevent this ungainly and not particularly successful practice (Gillies did not win), but later that week, the R&A Rules of Golf Committee issued a 'hope' that players would in future 'consider whether they were acting in conformity with the spirit of the game'. The foot-high tee seems to have disappeared, mainly because it would be an awkward thing to carry around in your pocket.

For most of us losing a tee is not a cause for wailing and gnashing of teeth. However, a French amateur golfer,

42

Paul Brewaeys, uses a tee with a string attached, and a 43
skewer on the other end of the string. He then sticks
the skewer into the ground, as well as the tee, so that if
he hits the tee out of the ground by the force of his drive,
it is restrained by the skewer and not lost. When I played
a round with him over the Queen's course at Gleneagles a
few years back, even the Scots were impressed with this
display of parsimony.

Another unusual tee peg was announced in 1932. The
Magnet Tee was a simple device consisting of a small
horseshoe magnet attached by a string to the tee. The idea
was that it would enable the golfer to pick up tees with
an iron club, without having to bend down. It failed to
catch on, firstly because most golfers do not consider bend-
ing down to pick up a tee too much of an athletic challenge, especially if they have already bent down to put the
tee into the ground. Secondly, most drives from the tee are
made with wooden clubs, which are not magnetic.

The superstitions which affect professional golfers
extend to the tees as well. Many golfers are suspicious of
white tee pegs, a problem which was exacerbated by the
cruel fate which befell Doug Sanders in the 1970 Open at

St Andrews. Sanders stood on the final tee needing a four to win the Championship. Suddenly, a spectator stepped forward from the gallery and offered Sanders a white tee peg, which he asked him to use as a mark of respect for Tony Lema, the golfer killed in an air accident in 1966, who had won the previous St Andrews Open, in 1964, using this same white tee. Sanders duly obliged, and on the green missed a 3-foot putt which would have won him the title. Instead he went into a play-off against Jack Nicklaus, which he lost. Sanders never won a major title, but whether that was entirely because he used white tees, we will never know.

44

DROPPED SHOTS

A number 9 wood
owned by Mary Lena Faulk, Baltimore, Ohio, 1960

Wooden golf balls used because of rubber shortage
Rhodesia, 1943

Waterproof golf club heads
patented by Weber, 1899

Ball thrown away instead of wrapping
Tom Whatson, 2nd hole, Barton-on-Sea GC, Hampshire, August 1976

Ball hit 250 yards with rubber-shafted driver
Willie Kidd, Interlachen GC, Toledo, Ohio, 1940s

£17,825 paid for golf ball
1845 'Feathery' ball made by Old Tom Morris, at Phillips auction, Kent, 1993

£16,100 paid for golf trophy
Spode bowl, inscribed 'Bow Of Fife Golfing Club, Prize Medal for 1814 Won by John Pitcairn Esq of Kenneard', bought by Mr Titus Kendall at Phillips, 1994

ROYAL AND

ANCIENT

3

Golf has been a royal game since it began. Nobody would wish to state categorically where it came from or how it began, but a likely story is that the game of golf was introduced to Scotland from across the Channel, by Flemish noblemen who accompanied Lady Maud de Lens, a great-niece of Count Eustace II of Boulogne, when her husband David I (1124–1153) ascended the Scottish throne in 1124. King David was, incidentally, the great-nephew of Duncan I, who had been murdered by Macbeth, the man who was determined to 'fight the course'.

In 1457, David's great-great-great-great-great-great-great-great-grandson, James II of Scotland (1437–1460), outlawed golf because he feared that it was luring people away from practising their archery, which he felt was a more efficient way of keeping the English out of Scotland. This theory was proven, incidentally, 470 years later when Art Young and Victor Bule, archers, defeated Harry Kennett and John Foge, golf professionals, in an 18-hole archery v. golf match at Lincoln Park GC in America, by 6 and 5. The golfers halved the first three holes, but after that the archers built a strong lead. Their accuracy around

45

the greens, where the archers never seemed to miss their six-inch target, was the main reason. The archers were two under par for the 13 holes played.

In 1491, James II's grandson James IV (1488–1513) also banned golf, but he repealed the law in 1503, when he married Henry VII of England's daughter, Princess Margaret, and began the genetic process which ended exactly one hundred years later in the union of the kingdoms of England and Scotland. On 3 February 1504, the Lord Treasurer of Scotland recorded an outlay of nine shillings, 'Item to Golf Clubis and Ballis for the King that he play it with'. By 1513, James IV's wife's sister-in-law Catherine of Aragon was writing to Cardinal Wolsey saying that in England everyone was 'busy with the golf, for they take it for a pastime'.

Mary Queen of Scots, granddaughter of James IV, is generally reckoned to be the first female royal golfer; indeed she lays claim to the title of first female golfer of whatever social status. She was reputed to have been playing golf 'in the fields beside Seton' a few days after the death of her second husband, Lord Darnley, in 1567. When their son James VI became James I of England, he brought the royal love of golf south to London, and the Royal Blackheath Golf Club, which dates from 1608, is reputed to have been established thanks to the interest of King James's sons, Henry and Charles. Prince Henry died of a fever aged 18 in 1612, but his younger brother Charles retained the Stuart passion for golf, to such an extent that he was golfing at Leith when told of the start of the Irish rebellion of 1641. He promptly abandoned his game, summoned his horse and rode off, the first but not the last time that a golf match has been curtailed because of civil disturbance. The rumour that he was six down with eight to play at the time seems to be unfounded. Seven years later King Charles emulated his golfing grandmother Mary by being beheaded, a fate that has not befallen any golfing royalty since that day. King Christian V of Denmark was killed in 1670 on what was to become Scandinavia's oldest golf course, but he was gored to death by a stag rather than beheaded, and the course itself was not built for another 228 years. The site of King Christian's death is near what is now the 16th hole of the Kobenhavns Golfclub.

47

King Hassan II of Morocco, an avid golf lover, has perhaps come nearer than anyone to becoming the third monarch after Mary and Charles to play golf and to be put to death, and he is the only ruler to have been imprisoned on one of his own golf courses. King Hassan had by 1971 built five personal golf courses: a floodlit nine-hole course in the palace grounds in Rabat, nine-hole courses at Fez, Meknes and Ifrane, and an 18-hole championship course at Skhrirat designed by Robert Trent Jones. It was at this last course that on 10 July that year an international tournament was taking place to mark the king's 42nd birthday. John Cook, a professional attached to Brickendon Grange GC, near Hertford, was one of several professionals who had flown out from the Open at Royal Birkdale to play in the tournament. He was at the king's birthday party, when suddenly Berber rebels broke in and shots were fired. The man standing next to Cook was hit, and fell dead in his arms. The Belgian Ambassador to Morocco, M. Marcel Dupret, was also killed. Cook was struck over the arms with a rifle butt and was injured, which would have been something of a problem for him on the course the next day. But the tournament was abandoned, like King Charles's in 1642, because of the insurrection.

Fortunately for golf fans everywhere, the rebels were incompetent. In the first moments of confusion, as shots burst balloons and sliced into birthday cake, the king managed to hide in one of the interior rooms off the throne room. He was eventually found but not recognized, and the rebels marched him with his hands at the back of his head to the golf course, where they put him with the rest of the prisoners. The rebel leaders, General Medbouh and Lt.-Col. Ababou, were both reported killed in the attack on the palace, and this seemed to take the wind out of the sails of the Berber separatists. An hour later, one of the junior officers who was checking the prisoners recognized King Hassan. Realizing which side of his bread was

buttered and fearing that it was about to land butter side down, he immediately knelt before his king and kissed his hand. He then confirmed that the only reason he and his colleagues had come to the palace was to protect the king, and the insurrection was over. King Hassan continues to build golf courses across his country, and the Royal Agadir Golf Club now hosts an early season European tour event. It is not known whether John Cook has ever been back for another royal birthday celebration.

The British royal family has maintained great interest in golf over the centuries, although on the monarch's birthday they have kept up the ancient tradition of Trooping the Colour rather than going in for the more dangerous Moroccan option of a golf tournament. James II, when Duke of York, partnered one John Paterstone, a shoemaker, in a round of golf against two English noblemen at Holyrood in 1681. The Duke and Paterstone won, and with his half of the winnings Paterstone was able to buy himself a house in Canongate in Edinburgh, called 'Golfer's Land'. The plaque on the wall bearing Paterstone's crest, a dexter hand grasping a golf club, with his motto, 'Far And Sure', can still be seen.

Paterstone, by winning without having to put up a stake, became the first golf professional, and keeping his prize home was much easier than for the Japanese professional Isao Aoki 298 years later. In the 1979 Suntory World Matchplay Championship at Wentworth, Aoki holed his tee shot from the 2nd tee in his match against the Australian David Graham. The prize for this achievement was a Bovis home at Gleneagles, worth £55,000. The Japanese tax authorities were not amused, however, and following John Paterstone's motto, they came from Far, and they were also Sure that Aoki had to pay tax on the value of his house.

In 1833, the Perth Golfing Society was the first to be granted the title of 'Royal', by King William IV, who was better known as 'the Sailor King' than 'the Golfer King'. Nevertheless, the next year he repeated his munificence by granting the 'Royal' title to the club at St Andrews, which thus became the Royal And Ancient.

By the turn of the twentieth century, golf had become the sport of kings, ex-kings, Grand Dukes and presidents. In 1904, King Edward VII, of whom it was diplomatically written 'nature had not made the King's figure suitable for driving a long ball', ordered that part of his land at Windsor be laid out as a golf course. The 1st tee was sited under a majestic cedar tree by the East Terrace Garden, right by the King's back door. At about the same time, a very small private pavilion was built on the cricket ground nearby, so that the King could watch the cricket in comfort and splendid isolation. After King Edward died in 1910, the pavilion was not used by his successor, King George V, and so permission was given for the little building to be used as a clubhouse for members of the Royal Household Golf Club. The only problem was that it was over half a mile from the 1st tee, built for the convenience of the King by the East Terrace Garden. On the other hand, it was only 250 yards from the 16th tee. So now the 16th tee is where the Royal Household GC begins its rounds. There is no good reason why the tees were never renumbered, but even today, visitors to the club have to be reminded to start at the 16th and work their way round to the 15th.

51

Edward VII's wife, Queen Alexandra, played at least once, with her daughter Princess Victoria, Sir Frederick Ponsonby and Sir Francis Knollys, on the private course at Sandringham. As Sir Frederick later wrote, 'the Queen seemed to confuse it with hockey and was under the impression that one had to prevent the opponent putting

the ball in the hole. This usually ended by a scrimmage on the green. She also thought that the person who got into the hole first won it, and asked me to hurry up and run between the strokes. It was very good fun, and we all laughed.' But it was hardly golf.

Queen Alexandra's son, George V, was not interested in golf either. As *Golf Illustrated* remarked on the death of the King in January 1936, 'golf was among the few sports with which HM King George V was not closely identified', but all the same, 'the memory of our late Gracious Sovereign will be found to be enshrined as passionately in the hearts of golfers as elsewhere'. His sons were far more keen. The Prince of Wales, later Edward VIII, was Captain of the R&A in 1922; the Duke of York, afterwards King George VI, was Captain in 1930; and the Duke of Kent completed a royal hat-trick of Captains in 1937. The present Duke of Kent's eldest son bears the title of Earl of St Andrews.

When Edward VIII abdicated in December 1936, *Golf Illustrated* showed its concern for the important things in life by refusing to comment on a mere constitutional crisis. 'It is not within our province to comment on the sad events of last week which finally resulted in the abdication of His Most Gracious Majesty King Edward VIII,' wrote the editor, 'but in welcoming his successor, His Most Gracious Majesty King George VI, we are fortunate in having in the new king one who has been identified with golf almost as closely as his brother and who, had he had greater opportunities for constant practice, might have been a very excellent player. Long live the king!' These days, his grandson and successor as Duke of York is the British royal family's leading golfer.

Continental kings and princes were just as eager to play golf as their British cousins. When Luxembourg's first golf course was opened in June 1936, HH Prince Felix of Luxembourg struck the first ball. King Leopold of the Belgians played in the Belgian National Championships of 1939, without success, and in the French Amateur Championship of 1949. Prince Rainier of Monaco is an avid golfer, as were the Shah of Iran and King Baudouin of Belgium. Even the Japanese royal family got into the act. In 1929, Princess Asaka of Japan was runner-up in the Ladies' Challenge Cup at Miyanoshita, Japan. The present Japanese Crown Prince, who studied at Oxford University, was often to be seen among the crowds at the Open Championships in his student years.

Being head of state, whether of royal blood or not, seems to bring out the golfing instinct in even the least likely individuals. Adolf Hitler presented a golf trophy for the Grand Prix des Nations tournament played at Baden Baden in 1936 to coincide with the Berlin Olympics. It was won by two British golfers, Harry Bentley and T.J. Thirsk. President Marcos of the Philippines held up play in the 1977 World Cup of Golf in Manila because he wanted to play 9 holes with some friends, and nobody dared to tell him that it would put out the entire day's schedule. Perhaps the delay was caused by his wife taking time to decide which pair of golf shoes to wear.

American Presidents are the keenest golfing heads of state. *Golf Illustrated* pointed out that 'considerable shock was expressed in the nation's press when it was learned that President Eisenhower was playing golf during the worst period of the U-2 crisis'. Some would say that as he was a good golfer but not a very good president, he was doing the right thing in a time of crisis. At least on the golf course he was far less dangerous than Gerald Ford, who routinely hit spectators with wild drives and approach shots. There have been no reported cases yet of him having hit somebody with a wild putt.

54

Without doubt, the president with the best golfing pedigree has been President George Bush. His paternal grandfather, Prescott Bush, was secretary of the USGA in the 1930s, and his maternal grandfather, George Herbert Walker, was president of the USGA when in 1921 he donated an International Challenge Trophy that became known as the Walker Cup.

President Clinton is less well known for his love of golf and golfers, a feeling that seemed to be mutual among members of the 1993 US Ryder Cup team, who were not keen to visit the White House before the competition. However, by the end of the year, the jogging President was including in some of his speeches an anecdote about Tom Watson giving him a golfing lesson. He has still some way to go before he understands that the golfing vote is vital to his prospects of re-election, though, or that most professional golfers are politically to the right of Attila the Hun. In 1993, President Clinton allowed the idea of a tax on golf to be floated, with predictably loud cries of anguish from America's 25 million golfers. US Ryder Cup player John Cook reacted by saying, 'We are examples of people who work hard and make lots of money, and he wants to take it away and give it to people who don't give a damn.' A White House spokesperson responded by saying, 'What's the Ryder Cup?' The Clinton proposal is not the first instance of such a tax being suggested. In the early 1950s, during the golf-mad Eisenhower's presidency, his Treasury secretary proposed a 20 per cent tax on all green fees, which he considered would bring in an annual revenue of $10 million. It did not progress through the legislature, perhaps because too many senators and congressmen were on the golf course at the time.

55

Among the kings of show business who have sponsored US professional events are Bing Crosby, Bob Hope, Andy Williams, Glen Campbell, Danny Thomas, Dinah Shore and Sammy Davis Jr. Bing Crosby, who played in the 1950 Amateur Championship at St Andrews, died on Friday 14 October 1977 after a round of golf at the then newly opened La Moraleja Golf Club just outside Madrid. Some reports rather unromantically say that he suffered a massive heart attack after completing only 17 holes, so that his widely reported final words to his partners Valentin Barrios and Manuel Pinero, 'That was a great round of golf, boys', were strictly apocryphal.

Bing Crosby may have proved the theme of the *New York Times* editorial of 3 March 1916, namely that golf is a dangerous game for old men, but Bing's partner on stage, screen and golf course, Bob Hope, would disagree. He had the satisfaction late in 1993 of scoring a hole-in-one at Palm Springs Golf Club, California, when aged 90. He hit a 4-wood which pitched a few yards from the pin, and rolled in. For the first time in many years, Hope was described as 'speechless', but he was reportedly humming a few bars of 'Thanks for the Memory' as he walked to the next tee.

Hope is not the oldest player to shoot a hole-in-one. There is a plaque on the 12th tee of the South Course at La Manga Club, on the Costa Calida in Spain, which records the feat of a Swiss golfer, Mr Otto Bucher, 'who on 13th January 1985 at the age of 99 years scored a hole in one here.' The hole is 130 yards long. Mr Bucher was only four months away from his 100th birthday. George Sehlbach, a 97-year-old golfer from Crystal River, Florida, achieved two holes-in-one in the same year, 1984. Seven years later, at the age of 104, he played 9 holes in 46.

The true worth of an older golfer is often reckoned by his ability to shoot his age. The Canadian golfer Arthur Thompson was probably the oldest to achieve this feat, when he shot 103 at Uplands GC, British Columbia, at the age of 103 in 1973. He died two years later. The

youngest player to achieve this feat is not recorded, although it is known that nobody under the age of sixty has managed it on a full-length course. The Rancho Bernardo Golf Club, in San Diego, California, claimed early in 1994 to have 24 members aged between 68 and 87, who had shot their ages a total of 175 times since 1975. An unnamed 80-year-old has done it 32 times since his 74th birthday. James Braid, born in 1870, was reported to have held a record of returning a birthday round with a score lower than his age until his 80th round. On 6 February 1950 at Walton Heath, he shot an 81. He died nine months later.

57

Playing on the highly lucrative Senior PGA Tour requires two things: proof that you are past your fiftieth birthday and plenty of loose change. The winners on the Senior Tour can make very big money (there was a total of over $26 million in prize money on offer in 1993), but all the same it has been estimated that you would need at least $75,000 to keep going on the Tour for a first year. Even the entry fee for the annual qualifying tournament is $2,000, non-refundable unless you are ill. So although there were five people who by the start of 1993 had each won over $3 million on the Senior Tour since it began in 1980, there were plenty more who came away from the Tour wiser but poorer. In 1993, 74-year-old Jerry Barber lost his Senior Tour card, but because he won the 1961 US PGA title, as a mere lad of 42, he has a lifetime eligibility on the standard US PGA Tour. So rather than give up competitive golf, as the more weak-livered Harry Vardon did when he failed to qualify for the Open

Championship in 1932, at the age of 62, Barber came back on to the regular Tour, with a devastating lack of success. Still, at least he gets a regular game of golf. And he was still a year younger than Old Tom Morris was when he last entered the Open, aged 75 in 1896.

When William Simpson of Exeter GC died in 1971, he was 99 years old. His obituary reported that he did not retire from golf until he was 95, but then he carried on playing snooker, which he considered an easier game, until past his 99th birthday.

Like snooker, golf is a sport where traditionally the old can hold their own against the young, but, as with snooker, traditions are changing. The young now play golf very well. The first time I played a round of golf with my then 12-year-old son, at Romney Warren GC, he shot a birdie 2 at the first par-3 he came to, thanks to a chip in from fifty yards. My rather stylish par was to no avail. Two 16-year-olds, Tyrell Garth Jr in 1941 and Ted Oh in 1993, have competed at a slightly higher level, in the US Open, although neither did so with as much success. Ted Oh is the son of the Taiwan-born Sadaharu Oh, who holds the record for most home runs in a Japanese professional baseball career. Young Ted shot a 76 and a 79, and will probably be back for more in years to come. Even so, it seems unlikely that he will develop as quickly as the British Ryder Cup player Barry Lane, who turned professional at the age of 16 in 1976, within two years of taking up the game.

When Francis Ouimet won the US Open in 1913, he was a 20-year-old amateur, and to win he had to beat

Harry Vardon and Ted Ray, two of the greatest players of the age, in a play-off. Despite his youth, Ouimet was twice the age of his caddie, 10-year-old Eddie Lowery. The combined ages of champion and caddie have never been lower in any subsequent national championship anywhere in the world.

Even Eddie Lowery was a couple of years older than Miss Marjorie Lewis, who at the age of seven and a half in 1923 was reported to have shown 'such marked ability that the Noragraph Film Company has filmed her at play'. The fact that her father was Earle R. Lewis, treasurer of the Metropolitan Opera House in New York, may explain the availability of cameras to record her efforts, but sadly Miss Lewis did not go on to great golfing things in adulthood. Bryan Rozier won his fourth major tournament in the United States in 1991 at the grand old age of five. *Golf* magazine discounted the precedent of Marjorie Lewis and nominated him as PGA Golfer of the Year for 2010 (when he will be 24). His main rival might be Thomas Would, a London lad born in 1992. His godfather, Paul Haxby, has placed a £10 bet with William Hill at 10,000 to 1 that young Thomas will win the Open by the time he is thirty, in the year 2022. Haxby was quoted as saying that Thomas's dad is a useless golfer, but he thought a £10 bet would be a nice present for him, as well as a reasonable incentive.

The oldest golfers are the dead ones, especially those who come back as ghosts. There are those who believe that, to be a half capable golfer, you have to sell your soul to the devil, and to them it is proof enough that golf is one of the more haunted sports, with ghosts on the fairways and halfway up the clubhouse stairs all over the world.

In the eighteenth century, Dame Margaret Ross of Balneil, wife of the Earl of Stair of Lochinch Castle, Stranraer, was believed to be a witch with terrifying powers. Her particular trick was to turn herself into a golf ball and deliberately roll out of line on the greens, to prevent people she disliked from winning. She also, when in the form of a golf ball, used to hop unbidden into the deepest recesses of the largest bunkers, just to annoy her opponents. I have a feeling that I have played with her without realizing it on more than one occasion. Once she was specifically said to have helped Sir Patrick Murray, then MP for Stranraer, to win at golf in return for a favour he had done for her.

The most famous ghost in golf is probably that of Marianne, Countess de Morella, who haunts the clubhouse at Wentworth. The Countess died in 1924, after a riding accident at the age of 93. Shortly after her death, the Wentworth estate, which had been her family home for three-quarters of a century, was sold to be turned into a golf course. When the club opened, her old home, ballroom and all, became the clubhouse. In 1993, extensive improvements and redecorations costing £10 million were put in motion, but almost immediately fences started collapsing, piles of concrete blocks were overturned and work was seriously disrupted by the ghostly figure in the corridors of the clubhouse. It took a visit from the Marquesa de Ter, the great-granddaughter of the Countess, to calm

things down. Apparently, the old lady was upset that things were no longer under her control, but after a brief discussion with her descendant, things returned to normal, or at least, to less paranormal.

Muffin Spencer-Devlin, the only professional golfer to have been named after a type of bread roll (or possibly a puppet mule), is also believed to be the only professional golfer to have been King Arthur in a previous life. Spencer-Devlin also claims to have been a Matabele king and an eighteenth-century dock worker. In this life, she has overcome a drug habit and manic depression, which are part of an unusual but probably not unhelpful background for a golf champion.

DROPPED SHOTS

Crown Prince wins Pro-Am
Prince Claus of the Netherlands, with Peter Oosterhuis, Dutch Open, 1974

Heir to throne reaches final of Parliamentary Handicap
Prince of Wales (later Edward VIII), in 1933. He beat Lady
Astor 2 and 1 in the semi-final

King represents his country at golf
King Baudouin (Belgium) v. France and Holland, 1958

Royal Golf Clubs overseas include
Australia: Royal Adelaide, Royal Canberra, Royal Fremantle,
Royal Hobart, Royal Melbourne, Royal Perth, Royal
Queensland, Royal Sydney
Belgium: Royal Antwerp, Royal Golf Club de Belgique, Royal
Golf Club des Fagnes, Royal Club de Hainaut, Royal Latem,
Royal Waterloo, Royal Zoute
Canada: Royal Colwood, Royal Montreal, Royal Ottawa,
Royal Quebec
Hong Kong: Royal Hong Kong
India: Royal Bombay (closed 1947), Royal Calcutta, Royal
Western India (closed)
Iran: Imperial Country Club, Tehran (closed after 1979)
Iraq: Royal Baghdad (closed after 1958)
Kenya: Royal Nairobi
Malaysia: Royal Johore, Royal Kedah, Royal Kelantan, Royal
Perak, Royal Selangor
Malta: Royal Malta
Morocco: Royal Club of Agadir, Royal Club d'Anfa, Royal
Dar es Salam, Royal Marrakech, Royal Mohammedia, Royal
Country Club of Tangier
Nepal: Royal Nepal, Kathmandu
Samoa: Royal Samoa, Upolu
Singapore: Royal Island, Royal Singapore (amalgamated 1963
to form Singapore Island Country Club)
South Africa: Royal Cape, Royal Durban, Royal Johannesburg,
Royal Port Alfred
Spain: Real Golf Bendinat, Real Club de Golf Las Palmas, Real
Club de Golf El Prat, Real Sociedad de Golf de Neguri,
Real Golf de Zarauz
Swaziland: Royal Swaziland
Zimbabwe: Royal Harare

Championship delayed by assassination of President
US Amateur Championship 1901, delayed for a week by the assassination of President McKinley on 14 September, eventually won 5 and 4 by Walter Travis

Archers v. golfers
Glenn H. Curtis and Sam Huff, a Seminole Indian, the archers, beat Mike Brady and Walter Andrews, Hialeah GC, Miami, 1923

Thrower v. golfer
B.H. Lyon v. E. McLennan, at North Foreland, Broadstairs, Kent, January 1949. McLennan, the golfer, beat Lyon, the cricketer, 5 and 4

R&A club member for 67 years
Mr D. Gillespie of Mountquhanie, Cupar, Fife, 1831 to 1898

R&A Captain goes on to become prime minister
Rt. Hon. Arthur Balfour, Captain of R&A 1894, winner of Parliamentary Handicap 1894, 1897 and 1910, Prime Minister July 1902 to December 1905

Six golfers, combined age 486 years, club membership 241 years
Two three-balls at Shooters Hill GC, London, 1960

Gross 66, net 64, aged 64
Mickey Roe, at West Middlesex GC, Southall, 1960

Quarter-finalist in Amateur Championship, aged 58
Beaumont Pease, later Lord Wardington, 1928

Amateur Champion, aged 54
Hon. Michael Scott, 1933

Ryder Cup competitor, aged 51 years, 22 days
Ray Floyd (US), 1993

Ryder Cup competitor and captain, aged 50
Ted Ray (GB), 1927

US Open Champion, aged 45
Hale Irwin (US), 1990

US Open Champion, aged 44
Ray Floyd (US), 1986

63

US Open Champion, aged 43
Ted Ray (UK), 1920

Open Champion, aged 44
Roberto de Vicenzo (Argentina), 1967

Hole-in-one, aged 2 years, 11 months
Mitchell Hollis, at the 50-yard 8th hole at The Eagles pitch
and putt course, Norfolk, 1991

Hole-in-one, aged 6
Cameron Hill, 7th hole at Rookery Park, Suffolk, May 1993
Mark Alexander, 6th hole at Chessington Golf Centre,
September 1989

Nine holes in 48, aged 3
'Tiger' Woods (US), 1978

Winner of national title, aged 13
Thuashni Selvaratnam, Sri Lankan Ladies Amateur Open
Championship, 1989

Taking part in PGA European Tour event, aged 15
Alexandre Henriques (Portugal), Madeira Island Open, 1994

Winner of national title, aged 16
Ronan Rafferty, Irish Close Championship, 1980

Ryder Cup player, aged 20 years, 36 days
Nick Faldo (Europe), 1977

HEALTHY, WEALTHY
AND WISE

G olf is meant to be good for you. Under normal circumstances, people are meant to come off the course feeling trim and relaxed, with a warm healthy glow suffusing their bodies. Golf is not as strenuous as rugby football, for example, but it requires enough physical effort to keep the body supple, without threatening the bodily well-being of the golfer. Or at least, that's the idea. Through the years, however, golfers have found ways of disproving the theory that golf is good for you, and have destroyed their physical and mental health on the golf course in a subtle variety of ways.

Many guides to health and fitness for golf have been written, but the image of elderly gentlemen puffing and hacking their way round the golf courses of the world remains the prevailing one to non-golfers. That image is reinforced by reports that professional golfers are among the least fit of all sportsmen, and that many cannot even touch their toes. But then again, they don't need to very often. Nevertheless, to compete on a professional tour, you have to be extremely fit. The schedule is unending, with the PGA European Tour in 1993 consisting of 38 events, each lasting a full week. The definition of 'Europe' for tour purposes includes North Africa, Madeira, the Arabian Gulf and Thailand, so the travelling alone would tax the strongest constitution. Four golfers, Mark Mouland, Jim Payne, Steven Richardson and Anders Sorensen, competed in 34 of the 38 events. Richardson holds the record for having competed most frequently in professional events in the 1990s, and it has paid off. By finishing in third place in the Turespana Masters Open de Andalucia in February 1993, he topped the £1 million winnings mark in only four seasons as a professional. This was the quickest million ever made on the European Tour.

Richardson, despite his iron constitution, has not always been good for the health of others on the course. At the Italian Open, at Modena GC near Bologna in May 1993, Richardson laid waste to a major cross-section of the gallery as he progressed to a final round of 69. He hit a spectator on the shoulder with his third to the 10th hole, scattered a group standing behind the green on the 11th, and caught an elderly male spectator on the ankle at the 13th. Spectating at major tournaments has always been a risky pastime, and there have even been suggestions that from time to time the players aim at the gallery in the knowledge that their ball will almost certainly rebound favourably off some poor fan who has paid good money to be used as a moving target, thus taking some of the risk out the more difficult approach shots.

Many of the more famous victims have been women. Bill Branch, partnering Ben Hogan in the 1953 Open at Carnoustie, hit a woman in the crowd with his second shot, from a bunker, at the 2nd hole in the first round.

The Australian Kel Nagle hit a woman in the crowd during his play-off with Gary Player for the 1965 US Open at St Louis, which probably hurt him more than it hurt her. The unfortunate lady needed stitches in her scalp, but Nagle lost the first prize money. Harry Secombe's drive from the 1st tee at Effingham GC, Surrey, in a Lord's Taverners charity event in the late 1970s hit a lady who thought she was safely hidden in a clump of trees well to the right of the correct driving line. She needed 18 stitches, but survived to be guest of honour at the following year's event. She then took up exactly the same viewing position, between the same trees, on the correct assumption that Sir Harry had never hit two identical shots in his life. Secombe had a taste of his own medicine when Air Vice Marshal Sir Ronald Ramsey Rae, who was chipping on to the 18th green, hit Sir Harry rather than the green. Secombe suffered from double vision for several days.

At the 1971 Open at Royal Birkdale, Lu Liang-Huan, popularly known by sub-editors who did not speak

Cantonese as 'Mr Lu', needed a birdie at the final hole to have a chance of tying Lee Trevino to force a play-off. His second shot was a wild hook which hit Mrs Lillian Tipping, 48, on the head and knocked her out. The ball, however, rebounded on to the fairway, and Mr Lu got his birdie. Unfortunately, so did Lee Trevino, who thus won the title without having to go to a sudden death play-off Happily, Mrs Tipping did not suffer sudden death either. She was taken to Southport Infirmary, and was discharged after having a number of stitches put in her scalp. Some years later, Mr Lu paid for her to have an all expenses paid trip to the Far East as compensation.

Occasionally a passer-by is felled by almost the right sort of golfer. At Letchworth Golf Club a greenkeeper was using his strimmer by the 14th green when he was felled by a vicious slice from a member who happened also to be a doctor from the nearby Queen Elizabeth II Hospital at Welwyn Garden City. As the unfortunate greenkeeper picked himself up, he was pleased to learn that his assailant, Mike Wilkins, was a doctor, but less impressed when he learnt that his speciality was obstetrics. He refused medical treatment.

What is the key to golfing fitness? Is it a diet of Golfer Oats, a product enthusiastically endorsed by golfers at the turn of the century and 'unequalled by either Home or American Manufacture. And Intrinsically The Cheapest'? Food is certainly an important part of a golfer's success rate, as Colin Montgomerie or Ian Woosnam, two of the great trenchermen of the pro game, would attest. Neither would go quite as far as Gary Player or Paul Eales have, though. Player famously appears to live on a diet of raisins, wheatgerm and bananas, with no alcohol or caffeine. English professional Paul Eales embarked on a five-year fitness plan in November 1993 which included a diet of six meals a day 'to provide the right kind of fuel to maintain my concentration level'. By February 1994, only three months into his fitness regime, he won the Extremadura Open in Badajoz, Spain, putting him way ahead of schedule. His nutritionalist also works with the Cambridge University boat race crew and Wigan Rugby League FC which implies that Eales will be a very big and powerful man indeed by the time he reaches the end of his Five Year Plan.

It is unlikely, therefore, that Paul Eales will ever blow his chances of a major title because of indigestion. In 1934, Henry Cotton was 10 shots ahead of the field as he went into the final round of the Open, held that year at the Royal St George's, Sandwich. All he had to do was to stay upright to win the championship. However, his lunch almost did for him. 'I was nearly beaten by indigestion,' he told the *Daily Mirror* afterwards. 'I had a very heavy lunch and every time I pivoted for a shot, I felt the effects of it.' He apparently began to perk up again after completing the first 12 holes in 55, and completed the round in 79, to win by five shots from Syd Brews of South Africa.

The American golf professional Tommy Bolt, winner of the 1958 US Open, also knew what problems could be caused by indigestion. Nicknamed 'Thunder' Bolt as much for his fiery temper as for his digestive problems, he had the unlovable habit of breaking wind noisily and violently on the tee as he prepared to drive off. Officials and gallery

were always claiming to be shocked by this, but since his idiosyncracy was well known, it might have been better for the gallery to watch him putt rather than drive. Eventually, Bolt was asked not to do it, but he was very upset, saying that officialdom was as usual trying to take colour out of the game.

Evil smells have caused problems to golfers as well as spectators. Colin Montgomerie shot a 76 in the first round of the Hong Kong Open on 24 February 1994, and put his worst competitive round for a year down to the fact that he is allergic to the smell of garlic and onions. A fertilizer was being used on the course to kill worms, and its smell, very reminiscent of garlic and onions, had made Montgomerie feel sick. This may explain why, despite finishing top money-winner on the European Tour in 1993, he never featured among the leaders in any of the tournaments held in France, although he had earlier overcome his serious nasal disability to come third in the Crédit Lyonnais Cannes Open in 1992.

Frenchman Antoine Lebouc is one of several professional golfers who suffer from that other nasal disability, hay fever: When he shot an 11 at the 12th hole in the second round of the Lancia Martini Italian Open at Modena on 21 May 1993, he blamed it on the feathery down from the pioppo trees which surround the green and which had set off his hay fever. The course officials vacuumed up the fluffy seeds, but it was too late for Lebouc, who failed to qualify for the final two rounds. The tournament was finally won by New Zealander Greg Turner, brother of New Zealand's most successful batsman of all time, Glenn Turner. The great American golfer Billy Casper suffered so many allergies that he refused to play in some tournaments where the courses had been sprayed, and for many years the only meat he could eat was buffalo.

71

Sam Torrance, the Scottish Ryder Cup golfer, deserves a chapter of his own to describe the obscure and often downright daft ways he has managed to injure himself. Although indigestion has not yet been recorded as one of his major problems, which helps to explain why a large gallery continues to follow him round at every event he plays, he spent most of 1993 suffering the slings and arrows of outrageous fortune: indeed, for some of the year he was wearing the slings caused by the arrows of outrageous fortune. He is the only professional yet known to have twisted his right shoulder watching television, and certainly the only one to have had to drop out of a tournament after colliding with a flowerpot while sleep-walking. He did his shoulder injury the night before the Open at Sandwich. 'I've never been in so much pain in my life,' he said. 'It was agony.' Nevertheless, he shot 72, 70, 72 and 71. He probably revised his opinion about the true

meaning of pain when, a month later, he crashed into a large flowerpot while sleepwalking the night before the Murphy English Open. His round the next day was a painful 78. 'It was agony on every shot,' said the battered Torrance. By the time the Ryder Cup came round at the end of September, Torrance was back in full health and in fine form, having been runner-up to Ian Woosnam in the Trophée Lancôme in Paris the previous week. However, he hurt the little toe on his left foot in making his opening drive in his foursomes match with Mark James against Lanny Wadkins and Corey Pavin, and before the outward half was over, he was in agony again. Overnight the toe went septic, and Torrance could play no further part in the fate of the Ryder Cup, unless a half in the singles for being absent counts as playing a part.

Golf is a mental as much as a physical pastime, especially if you drive round the course on a golf cart, so it is inevitable that many of the illnesses suffered by golfers prove to be psychosomatic. In January 1921, *Golf Illus-*

trated reported that 'London physicians are attacking a mysterious new disease, which afflicts golfers and is called neurophobia. In one case, a man could not stop waggling his driver at the ball before hitting it. He is now being treated by an expert in hypnotism.' Unfortunately, this particular symptom of neurophobia seems to have been highly infectious, as seventy years later practically every golfer in the universe seems to waggle his driver at the ball before hitting it. The article went on to report another case of a golfer who, having completed 9 holes in two under par, raised his driver to hit his 10th tee shot only to be seized by a temporary paralysis which rendered him completely incapable of completing his swing. Of course, no cure was found to this disease which, whatever its name, is still very much with us. That does not mean to say that on the 10th tees of courses around the world we will find golfers holding drivers aloft in paralysed desperation, but it does mean that most golfers can learn to blame almost anything but their own shortcomings for failing to break 100 yet again. In October 1932, a certain Dr L.J. Pollock briefly became the patron saint of bad golfers by proving, in an article in the *New York Times*, that hooks and slices could be blamed not on simple physical incompetence but on a 'labyrinthine reflex' of the mind. The great Harry Vardon had called this condition 'the jumps', and a few years later, Dr Pollock's reflexes became known as 'the yips', a term first used by 1927 US Open and 1931 Open Champion Tommy Armour. He was an endless clubhead waggler as he stood over the ball, waiting until he felt ready to hit it.

73

The yips are no longer a curiosity, although some of the methods to overcome them are. Bernhard Langer is the most famous recent example of a yips putter. He has suffered from and overcome the yips so well that nowadays his fellow professionals often cite him as the man they would like to see putting for their life. Langer grips his putter with his left hand and uses the right hand to clamp the putter handle to his left forearm, giving him a very stable putting action. The American professional Mac O'Grady simply switched from putting right-handed to putting left-handed, and this worked for him. Johnny Miller, who not only had yip problems but also injured his left hand in a motorcycle accident in the late 1970s, tried the broomhandle putter with his own individual style of gripping the handle under his arm to limit the movement of his wrists while putting. Leo Diegel, US PGA champion in 1928 and 1929, invented 'diegeling', a putting stroke with the elbows pointing out, which proved very successful in the 1929 Ryder Cup. Sam Snead, who has won more professional tournaments than any other golfer, including nine majors, tried a croquet mallet style of putting for a while, but this was declared illegal, so he adapted the method to one within the bounds of legality. He tends to push the ball in front of him, with the left hand at the top of the handle and the right hand as low down the handle as possible. Putting in defiance of the yips creates such a variety of curious styles that it is impossible to list them all: all golfers fear the onset of the dreaded yips just as actors fear stagefright and students fear examinations. Never take advice from a golfer on

74

your putting style. If the club you use is legal and you are holding it at the right end, then you can't look any dafter on the green than some of the best putters in the world. And, like them, occasionally you might hole a long one.

Some golfers play on despite the greatest of physical handicaps. Byron Nelson, who was undoubtedly the best golfer in the world in the mid-1940s, is a haemophiliac. Harry Gleadle, a 14 handicap player at Cleethorpes GC, won the club's Roots Cup competition in 1936, winning by 3 and 2 in the final, despite the handicaps of a club foot, a stiff left leg in irons and an unbendable knee joint, all the result of a First World War injury. Major Frank B. Edwards of Victoria, British Columbia, had an even worse war. Both his arms were shot away below the elbows in October 1916, at the Battle of the Somme. Somehow, despite this terrible disadvantage, he invented attachments for his artificial hands to enable him to play golf and billiards. The golfing attachment was for one hand only, and consisted of a clamped groove into which the club was inserted. He had to play one-handed, but given a fairly good lie, he could hit a ball about 100 yards, and it usually went very straight. He was described as playing 'a tolerably good game in the circumstances'.

Playing without hands is more difficult than playing without legs, which the late Sir Douglas Bader managed with such success that he reduced his handicap at one stage to 4. He had his legs designed to facilitate his golf, and always refused any help if ever he fell over on the course. Designing legs for the perfect golfer is quite a task, especially if one looks at the differences between the legs

of, say, Nick Faldo and Ian Woosnam, and asks what are the perfect dimensions for a golfer's legs? All the same, it does not stop surgeons from helping their patients wherever possible. Alistair Cooke, the golf-loving broadcaster whose 'Letter From America' is one of the longest-running programmes on BBC radio, was operated on in 1993 for a new knee joint. The original joint had deteriorated to such an extent that Cooke had become rather bow-legged, so when a new one was inserted, Cooke made sure that his doctors knew he was a golfer. Thanks to the addition of a little extra cement here and there, Cooke ended up with a joint which sets him up perfectly when he addresses the ball. Whether or not his handicap improves as a result remains to be seen.

Playing without eyes is even more difficult than playing without limbs. Capt. Sir Beachcroft Towse VC KCVO, who was blinded during the Boer War, was probably the first blind man to play golf regularly. He was already 37 years old when he lost his sight, but played on until shortly before he died, aged 84, on 21 June 1948. He was also President of the National Institute for the Blind and an accomplished fly fisherman, a sport which must be almost more difficult than golf for a blind person. At Golf de Chiberta, near Biarritz in southwest France, the blind golfer Joseph Echeverria played off a handicap of 5 in the early 1970s. The English Blind Golf Movement has for many years done tremendous things for blind adults and children, and the blind golfers play astonishingly well. Terry Wallace, who died in 1993, was a founder of the Movement and captained an English team of blind golfers against the United States at Wentworth in a Ryder Cup format match. Despite his own handicaps of diabetes, several heart attacks, cancer and total blindness, Wallace outdid his sighted counterparts by leading his English team to victory.

If you can survive injury, accident and psychological buffeting, then the rewards for the professional golfer are great. In 1993, the Zimbabwean Nick Price won $1,478,557 to top the United States money list, and even Ted Schulz at number 100 earned $164,260. In Europe, Colin Montgomerie led the Volvo Order of Merit with £613,682. Dave Stockton and Bob Charles both earned over $1 million on the US Seniors Tour, a figure that was matched by only five players on the regular tour, while Betsy King's $595,992 on the US Ladies' Tour would have placed her 27th on the men's list, above such famous names as Craig Stadler, Scott Hoch and Fuzzy Zoeller. The European Seniors and Ladies do not fare quite so well, but Tommy Horton's £56,935 to lead the Seniors list was probably more than he ever earned in a year on the European PGA tour. Laura Davies, who was second to Karen Lunn among the European Ladies with £62,938, was also 20th on the US Tour with a further $240,643. Bernhard Langer, by finishing 23rd on the American list and fourth in Europe, earned $626,938 and £469,569.

The money earned is increasing rapidly. Seve Ballesteros has been Europe's leading money-winner six times between 1976 and 1991. In 1976 he won just under £40,000, which was in itself virtually double what the previous year's leading money-winner Dale Hayes had collected; in 1991 he won £790,000, a twentyfold increase. Around thirty professionals have topped a career £1 million on the European Tour, and many more than that have won $1 million in America. Nick Faldo in 1993 became the first golfer to make over £4 million in total official earnings on the PGA European Tour, but the official earnings are only a small part of the story. In the same year he was listed by the *Sunday Times* as one the richest people in Britain, with a fortune estimated at over £20 million. Greg Norman, who took over from Nick Faldo as the world's number one early in 1994, was then earning an estimated £7 million a year from his investments in golf club manufacture and golf course design, quite apart from his phenomenal earnings on the golf course.

Even at the lower levels of golf, money is there to be made. Of course, if you wish to retain your amateur status, you must be seen not to make money out of golf or out of your fame as an amateur golfer, which was a rule the great Bobby Jones fell foul of after he retired from playing competitively. This was a problem which Jason Bohn had to consider when, in 1992, he took part in a charity golf competition at a golf club in Tuscaloosa, Alabama. A first prize of $1 million was offered to anybody who could manage a hole-in-one at the 135-yard 2nd hole. Bohn, then aged 19, succeeded, and had to decide whether to take the money and forfeit his amateur status, or carry on playing as an amateur. He no longer enjoys amateur status.

Large bets are, of course, commonplace in golf. Greg Norman financed his first trip to Europe by betting on his skill at golf, and Ray Floyd and Lee Trevino, among many others, have played for very high stakes indeed early in their careers. However, the best bets are the simplest. When Alan Doxford played himself in as Captain of the Hartlepool Golf Club, in 1981, he took the traditional bets of golf balls with his fellow members. The bet was that he would not get a birdie 3 at the first hole after his drive-in. Doxford, a 1 handicap player, was confident that the 253-yard par-4 was a straightforward birdie hole for

him, and he took all bets. He easily managed it, with a drive, a chip and a putt, and collected 148 balls.

The early golfers at Blackheath seem never to have gone out on to their course unless there was a decent wager involved. On 3 September 1791, it was recorded that 'Mr Hamilton bets Mr Innes one Gallon Claret that he beats him next Saturday, giving him 28 strokes in 4 rounds,' which at Blackheath meant 20 holes, not 72. A week later, the club's chronicle showed that Mr Innes had lost. But gambling was not necessarily good for the health of the members. On 26 May 1821, we learn that 'the melancholy event of this day, viz. the sudden death of Mr Campbell at the moment of his conclusion of his bet against the Secretary, was noticed in solemn silence.' Three years later, in 1824, Mr Robertson challenged Mr Black senior 'for a gallon of whisky, Mr Black giving Mr Robertson two strokes a hole, which Mr Black accepts solely for the good of the club, on account of it being for whisky.' Mr Black senior lost the bet.

In 1932, a certain Dr Frederick Ream of New York played his fellow physician Dr Vincent Callahan for a curious prize. The loser had to bath a goat. Callahan lost, and *American Golfer* magazine printed a picture of the good doctor plus goat, tin bath and a bar of soap. All this goes to show that not all golf is designed to make one healthy, wealthy or even wise.

DROPPED SHOTS

Foot injury prevents participation in tournament
Vera Ramsay (GB), before American Ladies' Championship, 1915

Percy Alliss (GB), before Ryder Cup, 1929
Sam Torrance (Europe), during Ryder Cup, 1993

Golf team involved in railway accident
Oxford University team, on the way to Wimbledon, 1878

Eventual winner of tournament hits spectator with ball
Bob Andrews, match v. Tom Morris Sr at Prestwick, 1860s
Bobby Jones, Amateur Championship at St Andrews, 1930
Greg Norman, Suntory Matchplay at Wentworth, 1980

Leg broken while playing in the Open
Richard Boxall, while driving from the 9th tee in the third
round, Royal Birkdale, 1991

81

*Leg broken while playing in European Teaching Professionals
Championship*
Russell Weir, while driving from the 7th tee, Broeckpolder,
Holland, 1991

Left leg and right ankle broken in skiing accident
Phil Mickelson (US), 1994

*Knee, shattered in accident, having to be rebroken and reset
three times*
Patty Berg, 1942. She won the Western Open in 1943

Golfer falls twelve feet out of oak tree
Roger Chapman, at Forest Park, November 1993

*Ryder Cup golfer falls from tree as a child and is therefore
unable to straighten left elbow*
Calvin Peete (US)

*Golfer falls three stories off multi-storey driving range,
breaking left leg*
Toshiaki Yujima, at Gunma, Japan, 1989

Golfer wins 1954 US Open despite withered left arm
Ed Furgol (US)

Golfer wins tournament despite withered left arm from polio
Larry Hinson (US), New Orleans Open, 1969

*Golfer almost qualifies for 1914 Open at Troon, despite having
no left arm*
Yves Botcazou (France), assistant at Golf de la Boulie, Versailles

Golfer misses a year's golf after lawn-mower accident
James Cook, British Youth Champion 1987, hurt his wrist in 1990

Golfer loses 40 per cent of feeling in left hand in accident with glass door
Jay Sigel (US), June 1963

Rib broken by falling on golf ball in pocket
Liam Higgins, Waterville GC, Co. Kerry, September 1992

Golfer strains back stooping to pick up razor while shaving, on morning of last round of US Open
Craig Wood, Fort Worth, Texas, 1941. He played in a truss and won the title

Golfer affected by myalgic encephalomyelitis (ME)
Daren Lee, Open Championship at Muirfield 1992, where he finished as top amateur

Net 72 in Stage Golfing Society's Monthly Medal despite a bleeding ulcer
Michael Balfour, March 1960

Course record broken in the afternoon, following wisdom tooth extraction in the morning
Fred Daly, Letchworth, 1950

Hole-in-one by one-armed player
Lester P. Edge, 145-yard 10th hole at Spokane Country Club, 13 May 1927
J.S. Potter, 4th hole at Wooden Bridge, Co. Wicklow, 1938
George Jackson, 13th hole at Shortlands GC, Kent, 1942
Ray Woodhouse, 8th hole at Mapperley GC, Nottingham, May 1994

$1 million golf club as prize in tournament
Lawrenceburg GC, Kentucky, given as first prize in 3,000 entry competition, 1994

IN BREACH OF THE RULES

5

Golfers are not like the rest of the population, with some good and some bad. All golfers are honest people, by definition. They have to exercise the utmost self-control on the course, so naturally they behave equally well off the course. It is therefore more than a curiosity, it is an almost unimaginable aberration that they should ever come into contact with the forces of the law. All the same, there are a few cases of golfers who have let themselves and their fellow golfers down, by getting into legal difficulties.

Hitting people with a golf ball is the most common crime perpetrated by golfers. Usually little harm is done, and a mumbled 'I'm very sorry' does the trick, even if it is often followed by an even more mumbled 'Stupid fool. That would have reached the green if he hadn't been in the way.' Sometimes, however, the hittees take matters further. In November 1932, in the epoch-making case of Simpson v. Fiero, an American court ruled that a golfer is immune from damages for injury to his own caddie, but liable if he hits somebody else's caddie. But in 1951, a New Jersey court threw out a damages suit brought by a man hit in the head by a golf ball. The golfer admitted that he had not shouted, 'Fore!' but the jury decided that he had shouted, 'Look out!', and that was enough.

In Florida, it is worth while shouting something more polite if you want to play through a slow fourball. At Sabal Palm Golf Club in the summer of 1993, John Tennyson and Howard Polley were so frustrated by the slow play of Hugo Torres and his colleagues that they played through at the 7th hole without so much as a nod of acknowledgement. Torres, quite justifiably, considered this a terrible breach of golfing etiquette, and an argument began. By the time it had ended, Torres had hit Tennyson on the back with his pitching wedge (although most professionals would recommend a sand iron in similar circumstances), and Tennyson's partner Howard Polley had taken a swing at Torres. The club used is not recorded, but it would certainly have been an air shot had not Torres blocked it with his arm. The club broke and Torres then stabbed the unfortunate Polley in the neck with the broken shaft of his own club. Polley and Tennyson were taken to hospital, and Torres was taken to the police station, so none of the golfers finished their rounds. Torres was

released on $10,000 bail, making it quite possibly the most expensive seven holes ever played.

In White Plains, New York, in 1950, there was a case in which a man was suing for damages for the loss of an eye when he was hit by a golf ball. The American Walker Cup player Willie Turnesa, British Amateur Champion of 1947 and US Amateur Champion a year later, appeared as an expert witness for the defence. The judge refused to allow Turnesa to estimate the speed of a golf ball from the tee, but instead allowed him to demonstrate in court. A canvas sheet was put up in court and for ten minutes Turnesa drove balls into it. He made so much noise that people ran into the courtroom from all over the building, fearing that shooting had broken out. Whether or not this display of hard hitting actually helped the defence's case, it must have compromised Turnesa's amateur status if he received any payment for his appearance as an expert witness.

In September 1993, Charles D. Carey entered a charity golf competition at the Hanging Tree Golf Club in Noblesville, Indiana, but his conduct there was anything but noble. Acting on a tip-off, plain clothes detectives followed him round all 18 holes, and when he handed in his card showing a 67, they arrested him. By their count he had taken 80 strokes, not 67, and was thus guilty of the theft of his prize, a $50 gift voucher. He was taken to Hamilton County Jail in Noblesville, where reporters were informed that Carey had also won a $500 set of golf clubs by ignoble means some time before the incident at Hanging Tree. Carey faced a maximum sentence of a $10,000 fine and three years in prison, not to mention an official revision of his handicap.

Willie Park Sr spent the night in gaol after winning the first Open Championship in 1860, but this did not stop him winning the title three more times over the next fifteen years. In fact, Open Champions seem to thrive on brushes with the law. After a round of golf at Worplesdon GC, at Woking in Surrey, former Open Champion Alf Padgham and England cricketer Alf Gover were driving down West Hill in Putney when they were caught in a police speed trap. Gover, who was driving, was giving his name and address to the officer when Padgham remarked that it was a pity that such a lovely day's golf had to end that way. The policeman looked closely at him and then said, 'You must be Alf Padgham.' There then followed several minutes of impromptu coaching by Padgham on how to cure a hooked tee shot, using a driver taken from the boot of the car. At the end of the session, under the street lights, the policeman came over to Alf Gover and tore up his

notes, saying, 'You just watch your step in future, sir.' A case of two Alfs getting out of a hole.

Getting into the hole was more Ray Floyd's problem. He once left his putter in a restaurant with a note saying, 'If anybody decides to steal this putter, let them.' But of course, no golfer would steal a putter, even with an invitation to do so. The message and the putter were found by a journalist. Ben Crenshaw was equally unlucky. He lost the putter he wanted to keep. Little Ben, as it was affectionately known, had been given to him by his father in 1969 and Crenshaw had used it in every tournament he had won. It was stolen from the boot of Crenshaw's car in February 1992, but its loss did not stop his winning ways, as he notched up further Tour victories in 1992 and 1993. Leslie Madison, an American professional, came across another professional who was clearly no golfer, when he had his pocket picked by an unknown member of the gallery during the final round of the 1936 US Open at Baltusrol. The wallet contained $55. Madison finished in 55th place and so failed to win back any of the cash so deftly taken from him. And take pity on the unfortunate Mr J.E. Fraser, who swept all before him in the qualifying round of the Atlantic Coast Championship, in May 1932. As he stepped forward to receive the watch which was to be his prize, the organizers had to admit it had been stolen.

As the popularity of golf roughly coincided with the invention of the motor car, it is not surprising that their histories should be inextricably interwoven. One of the first specialist clubs to be invented was the 'track-iron', a forerunner of the niblick, which itself is a forerunner of the high irons and pitching wedge. The track-iron was used for getting balls out of cart tracks, which in the 1850s tended to be an integral part of the links. Over one hundred years later, although most vehicles had been banished from most golf courses, the suggestions book at the Royal St George's Club at Sandwich records the rather wistful suggestion that 'members refrain from driving their cars up and down the practice ground, especially for the purpose of retrieving their balls'. And it is not only the courses which get damaged by motor vehicles. In 1980, the clubhouse at Bolton Old Links GC was destroyed when it was hit by a tanker full of tar, which went out of control. In 1991, thieves stole a JCB digger near Liphook GC in Hampshire, and drove it down the 4th fairway towards the clubhouse. When they reached their target, they smashed a large hole in the clubhouse wall and departed with the safe, which contained about £2,000. A similar trick was tried at night at Sene Valley GC in Kent a year or so later, but the thieves got their vehicle stuck in a bunker and had to abandon the raid.

On many if not most courses in the United States, golf carts are compulsory, but more powerful vehicles, like JCB diggers, are strictly banned. This is bad news for hackers. The nearest I have so far come to a hole-in-one was at a par-3 hole at a course near Lisbon, when my tee shot, overhit and oversliced, hit the raised shovel of a mechanical digger to the right of the fairway, and rebounded to within six inches of the pin. I sank the putt for a very fine birdie. When David Fitt, a 25-year-old window cleaner, took his Austin Montego for a drive in Moretonhampstead, Devon, the golfers at the Manor House Hotel course were not impressed. At Exeter Crown Court, Fitt pleaded guilty to two charges of dangerous driving, three charges of criminal damage and one charge of driving while over the legal limit of alcohol. His criminally damaging driving all took place on the golf course, including a 360° handbrake turn on the 4th green. Ignoring the shouts of the players, he was finally stopped after a chase which involved seven police cars and a helicopter. In his defence, the court was told that 'it is a strange case. He can recall very little of what happened.' The arresting officer, PC Ian Walker, said that 'Fitt said he hated fat bastards who played golf. It was a good advert for the Montego.' We would not all necessarily agree that doing handbrake turns on the 4th green constitutes a good advertisement for any vehicle, even a rightly discontinued model like the Montego.

Philip Kelly of Rowley Regis, Staffordshire, might also consider that golfers are fat bastards, but at least in his

case, he saved money rather than lost it. Mr Kelly lived next door to a golf club, and in 1971 had his rates reduced as a result. He claimed that golf balls had smashed his windows three times, had dented his car and rebounded with monotonous regularity from the walls of his garden. He took 132 golf balls to the Valuation Panel in support of his appeal. If he had lost, he could at least have made a few pounds by selling the balls back to the club members.

90   Another less legal way of making money out of golf club members is to rob them while they are playing. Some would say that the green fees these days are daylight robbery, but even the green fees of £40 or £50 at some of the smarter courses in Britain are cheap compared with what can happen in Thailand. At the Siam Country Club just outside Bangkok, bandits used routinely to cut across the golf course as a short cut between their camps and their principal hunting grounds in Bangkok. Golfers were often asked to make up any shortfall in earnings that the bandits might have suffered after a bad day in the city, but often they left the golfers alone, provided they did not get in the way of any misdirected long irons out of the rough. In 1990, Oliver Anthony, 60, was playing at the Davy Crockett Golf Club in Memphis Tennessee (which is incidentally the only club named after a top ten hit record in a city after which another top ten hit song has been named). As he prepared to drive off at the 8th tee, he was held up at gunpoint by a passing criminal. It was only later in the round that he noticed a tear in his trouser pocket, and a bullet embedded in the spare golf ball he carried in it.

At Leeuwkop Golf Club just north of Johannesburg,

there are more than a few passing criminals. This is because the 18-hole course is within the walls of Leeuwkop Prison, an institution that plays no small part in the South African government's uncompromising 'correctional services' policy. The caddies, happy to work for a few rand per round, are the inmates. This is not a relaxed open prison where you might find jaywalkers and captains of industry on caddie duty. In a recent fourball, the somewhat nervous visiting golfers found that their caddies included a Mandrax dealer and Ephraim, who was in for murdering a fellow commuter at a bus stop. Few of his club selections were questioned by the golfers.

The laws of the land, however, are not as important to golfers as the Rules of Golf. Within just 34 Rules, preceded by a most important section on Etiquette and another containing 48 Definitions from 'Addressing The Ball' to 'Wrong Ball', all the drama of golf is revealed. Oh, and there are three Appendices as well, on Local Rules, Design of Clubs and The Ball. The number of books available which explain the Rules to mere mortals are significantly greater than the number of Rules in the Rule book, and still there are examples of on the spot adjudication which rival ice dancing judgements in their subtlety and incomprehensibility. In 1993, Haydn Selby-Green called for rulings no fewer than 21 times in European PGA events, but this obsession with not infringing the Rules did him little good. He ended up in 150th position in the Tour rankings, with a gross income of only £21,138.

Selby-Green would have had even more trouble in the days before the Rules were unified by the R&A. Sir Walter

Simpson, Bt., Captain of the Honourable Company of Edinburgh Golfers, wrote in 1888 that even the most basic of golfing events meant different penalties at different courses. Striking Opponent or His Caddie at St Andrews, Hoylake and Westward Ho! in those days meant that you lost the hole, except on medal days, when it counted as a rub of the green. The Bembridge GC code, on the other hand, stated that on a medal day you could replace without penalty. I am fairly certain it was the ball that one was allowed to replace without penalty, rather than the Opponent or His Caddie who had been struck.

There are times when interpreting the Rules requires oracular skills of a high order. In 1978, a golfer at Royal St George's holed a long putt, but as he stepped forward to pick his ball out of the hole, the ball jumped on to the green, closely followed by a frog which had been relaxing in the cup. Had the golfer holed out or not? The question was eventually referred to the R&A Rules of Golf Committee, who decided that the golfer had not holed out, because the ball had obviously never hit the bottom of the

92

cup. By that time it was too late to replay the hole. At Hunters Hill GC in 1911, a player who was allowed a free drop in accordance with a local rule, dropped it over his shoulder and into his golf bag. Was he allowed another drop without penalty? This question was also lodged with the Rules of Golf Committee, who decided that he was. By the time the ruling was announced, either the player and his partners had taken the Rules into their own hands, or else there would have been a very long queue of golfers waiting to play through.

93

Local rules are the bane of a golfer's life, although sometimes they do work to his advantage. The American magazine *Fairway* reported in February 1927 that 'British golfers are puzzling over a freak hole-in-one. A player's tee shot rolled past the flag, up the sloping bank at the back of the green and into a rabbit hole. By a local rule, the ball was picked out and dropped without penalty. It rolled down the sloping green and into the cup.' When Claudine Gros and Brigitte Varangot of France were playing a foursome against a British pair at West Herts GC in April 1960, their ball disappeared down a foxhole. Contemporary reports state that 'a caddie gallantly recovered it', but we do not know if they were penalized. Mlle Varangot went on to win more Amateur national titles in Europe than almost anybody else during the 1960s, so her game was certainly not adversely affected by this encounter with a fox.

Wars, riots and civil commotions can create difficulties for even the most dedicated golfer, but the round must go on. In Lucknow in the autumn of 1992, when England's cricketers were touring the subcontinent at a time of unrest between Moslems and Hindus, players and pressmen played golf, but only with each fourball protected by six soldiers armed with submachine-guns. During the Second World War, many clubs had to introduce local rules to take the situation into account. At Richmond GC, the local wartime rules included the concession that 'in competitions during gunfire or while bombs are falling, players

may take cover without penalty for ceasing play'. The committee had the safety of their members in mind when they arranged for the positions of known delayed action bombs to be marked by red flags 'at a reasonably but not guaranteed safe distance therefrom'. The job of placing those red flags was not one for which people readily volunteered. But at least they went on to allow that 'A ball moved by enemy action may be replaced, or if lost or destroyed a ball may be dropped not nearer the hole, without penalty.' At Folkestone GC, the wartime rules included the rather grudging allowance that 'a ball may be lifted and dropped if in a bomb hole in the rough, but not if the bomb hole is in or part of a recognized hazard.' So if you sliced your drive and just caught a bunker by the side of the fairway, which then turned out to be fifty feet deep thanks to an overnight bombing raid, you just had to play out of the hazard, however unrecognizable it might have been compared with the day before. They breed tough golfers in Folkestone.

Falling foul of the more regular rules is an occupational hazard. Tom Watson, who has written a book on the Rules, received three penalty strokes on one hole during the first round of the 1993 Masters. His second shot landed in a flower bed (of which there are plenty at Augusta) and he decided it was unplayable, so dropped for a penalty stroke. His ball rolled on landing, but it did not roll two club lengths, so Watson was wrong to drop again. Another stroke lost. Finally, as he swung, the ball moved and Watson lost yet another shot. He still got down in 7 for the par-5 hole, and finished the round on 71.

Golfers frequently call foul against themselves, as David Frost of South Africa did in first round of the Million Dollar Challenge at Sun City on 2 December 1993. On the 10th green, the ball moved as Frost addressed a 20-centimetre putt, so he called the foul on himself, incurring a one-shot penalty. However, he then neglected to place the ball back in its original position, and thus incurred a further one-shot penalty. The ball had not moved more than a millimetre anyway, and neither Frost nor his playing partner Bernhard Langer knew about the replacement rule, so they could only agree with a tournament official, the aptly named Dennis Brayns, who described Rule 18–2 as 'one of the cruellest in the game'. The great Bobby Jones called foul on himself during the 1925 US Open at Worcester, Massachusetts, when he caused his ball to move while addressing it in the rough around the 11th green. When he was commended for his sportsmanship, Jones commented, 'That's like praising a man for not robbing a bank.'

Jamie Spence was not trying to rob the bank when he failed to call a foul on himself at Castelgandolfo on 15 April 1993, but he would have avoided disqualification if he had done. At the 15th hole in the first round of the

Roma Masters, Spence took an incorrect drop, a mistake which was made with the full agreement of his playing partners. He signed for a 67, but several hours later a television viewer telephoned to say that Spence had been in breach of the Rules, so Spence was disqualified. Debate raged as to whether he had to be automatically disqualified – the general opinion being that he did not – but an even greater debate raged about what sort of a golf fanatic it was who is so determined to show off his superior knowledge that he will bring about the disqualification of an honest golfer. The use of television to help decide questions of Rules is also a doubtful area. So few shots within a tournament are actually televised that the leading players, who are the ones most often followed by the cameras, are bound to be most disadvantaged. Maybe this should be seen as an extra layer of handicapping for the best players, but all it really does is create a generation of Haydn Selby-Greens, hardly daring to play the next stroke without official advice for fear of an unexpected penalty.

Television is not the only guilty medium, of course. Joakim Haeggman of Sweden was fined £500 for swearing loudly at the 13th hole during the first round of the Dunhill British Masters at Woburn on 3 June 1993. Fair enough, you might say, except that the fine was not imposed on him until a week later at the Honda Open at Gut Kaden, Hamburg, because PGA European tour officials did not know about the incident until they read about it in the *Guardian*. Haeggman should never have learned to swear in English. If he had stuck to Swedish, not even the *Guardian's* golf correspondent would have understood.

Robert Lee managed to pick up a fine for bad language when it was not even he who spoke the words, and they were not spoken on the golf course. On the final day of the European Tour's Qualifying School tournament in Montpellier in November 1993, Lee woke at 5.30 a.m. with the awful realization that his golf clubs were locked in the clubhouse at La Grande Motte. They may have been safe, but they were in the wrong place. Lee was due to tee off at Massane, over five miles away, within an hour or two. In seeking to get hold of his clubs, he managed to set off the burglar alarm at La Grande Motte clubhouse, but by the time he had persuaded the gardener to let him get his clubs, the 6.30 bus to Massane had left without Lee and his caddie, known as 'Edinburgh Jim'. They finally managed to get a lift to Massane with a Tour official, in a dash reminiscent of that made by Fred Simpson in a taxi from Edinburgh to Muirfield for the 1926 Amateur Championship final against the American Jesse Sweetser. Simpson had lost 6 and 5, but Robert Lee did much better. He shot a 69 to qualify easily, but not before Edinburgh Jim had sworn so colourfully at the organizer of the Tour bus that Lee was fined £100.

Anders Forsbrand showed far more restraint when he earned himself a two-stroke penalty for taking off his sock and shoe at the 1993 Masters. On the third day his ball landed in Rae's Creek by the 13th green, and so he took off his footwear in order to play the ball from the shallows. To give himself balance, he leant on his golf club as he bared his feet, without realizing that he was just inside the yellow line which showed the boundary of the hazard. A

two-stroke penalty for grounding his club in a hazard was his fate. He finished the round with a 75, but came back on the final day with both shoes on throughout the round, to shoot a 66 and end up with a share of 11th place.

Occasionally, even golfers feel the need to show their anger. In Taipei, the capital city of Taiwan, traffic was stopped on 21 December 1993, not by the flood of Christmas shoppers but by a march of ten thousand golfers, caddies and golf course owners protesting against a government crackdown on unlicensed golf courses on the island. It did no good, apart from allowing those specialists in cross-country golf to get in a little extra practice. The government did not change its views, but it has bitten off more than it can chew. It is not just the courses that are unlicensed: the clubs, balls, clothing and even the instruction manuals are all routinely pirated in a country which until recently has not believed in international copyright conventions. The cheapest Ping putters, the most believable fake Dunlop 65 balls and the gaudiest of Payne Stewart plus fours have all been made in Taiwan.

DROPPED SHOTS

100,000 balls stolen from a 9-hole course
Moscow, 1990

Lead stolen from roof of clubhouse
Eden Course, St Andrews, 1960

Tournament lost by treading on ball
Roger Wethered (UK, amateur) lost 1921 Open Championship
at St Andrews in play-off with Jock Hutchison (US). Play-off
only necessary because Wethered dropped a shot by treading
on his ball at the 14th hole in the third round

Hole lost in Ryder Cup because caddie asked what club opponent used
Bernard Gallacher (UK) v. Arnold Palmer (US), 7th hole at St
Louis, 1971

Hole lost in Ryder Cup because caddie picked up the ball
Gardner Dickinson (US) v. Harry Bannerman (UK), 7th hole at
St Louis, 1971

Stroke lost by dropping mashie on ball
Harry Braid v. E.W.E. Holderness, British Amateur
Championship, Hoylake, 1920

Two strokes lost for not understanding English
Martin Posse (Argentina), 3rd round of the 1939 Open
Championship at St Andrews, for not understanding the local
rule not to ground club in the roadside grass at the 17th

Strokeplay play-off conceded at 35th hole
by Arnaud Massy (France) v. Harry Vardon (UK), Open
Championship, Royal St George's, 1911

Disqualified for moving an advertising hoarding
Nick Price (Zimbabwe) in 1992 Million Dollar Challenge, at
Sun City, South Africa

Disqualified from US Open for arriving ten minutes late on tee, still wearing street shoes
Severiano Ballesteros, Baltusrol, 1980

Disqualified from Open for using an illegal putter
C. Rotar (US), at Royal St George's, 1949

Open Championship won despite replacing ball in the wrong place on the final green
A.D. 'Bobby' Locke (South Africa), St Andrews, 1957

Open Championship won after breaking into pro shop to retrieve clubs
A.H. Padgham (UK), at Hoylake, 1936

Major championship lost because of incorrect scorecard
Roberto de Vicenzo, 1968 Masters at Atlanta, Georgia

Disqualified for teeing off early
Johnny Bulla, US Open, Fort Worth, Texas, 1941

US Women's Open title lost because of incorrect scorecard
Mrs Jacqueline Pung, 1957 Women's Open at Winged Foot GC, Mamaroneck, New York

National championship restarted after two rounds when it was discovered that tee markers had been moved
Spanish National Championship, 1993

Title almost lost thanks to incorrect information given by officials
Julie Hall (Felixstowe Ferry CG), 1993 English Ladies' Amateur Strokeplay Championship at King's Norton. Miss Hall finally beat Kate Egford (Hockley GC) in a play-off despite having thought she had won outright

Disqualified for 20 years for 'putting irregularities'.
David Robertson (Dunbar), 1985

Disqualified for three years for altering scorecard
Johan Tumba (Sweden), 1991

Disqualified from 1991 European Tour for incorrectly replacing ball
Constant Smits van Weasberghe (Holland)

Disqualified from Asian Tour for adjusting scorecard
Vijay Singh (Fiji), 1983

ANIMAL LOVERS

6

Golfers and animals are not meant to get involved with one another; but they do. The golf course is often built on common ground, and even the most private of golf clubs cannot keep out the rabbits, snakes and crows that seem to crop up at the most inconvenient moments of the round. Some clubs make efforts to keep the wildlife in its proper place, with instructions to members as to what to do when encountering the local fauna. 'Do Not Feed the Alligators' is the sign at the Marriott Hotel golf course in Orlando, Florida, but South Africans Jurie Visagie and Ben Fouchee came too close for comfort to the course crocodile as they played the 3rd hole in the third round of the Zimbabwe Open at Harare at the end of

1993. Visagie finished with an 80, remarking that he was lucky still to be in one piece after almost treading on the crocodile's tail as he crossed a bridge. Fouchee was less affected by the reptile's antics and shot a 71, perhaps because the crocodile went not for him but for his wife, who was caddying for him.

A woman wearing a red sweater was chased by a slightly less dangerous animal, a bull, during a match between John Panton (UK) and Otway Hayes (SA) at Houghton GC, Johannesburg in 1951. The players suddenly heard a scream and saw the bull, horns lowered and fully primed, lumbering towards her. She avoided disaster by hiding behind a tree and putting her mackintosh on over her pullover. The bull ambled off without causing further alarms. Dan McDonald, President of the Lakeside Country Club, Tacoma, Washington, had a more enjoyable encounter with cattle on the course. He was playing with Justice De Witt M. Evans at his club in 1915, when, on the 1st hole, McDonald's second shot was sliced, and struck a friendly cow that had invaded the golf course. The cow was obviously upset by the blow, though not seriously hurt, and kicked out at the ball as it fell to the ground. The ball flew on to the green, and Mr McDonald holed the putt for a birdie 3.

This co-operative cow is perhaps less typical of the wildlife encountered on golf courses than the more belligerent crocodile that went for the unfortunate Mrs Fouchee. More golfers seem to report their scores being hindered than helped by these living and often very loose impediments. There are exceptions, of course. According to *Golf*

Illustrated in 1949, Miss Mary Faulkner of Augusta, Georgia even went so far as to use her dog as caddie. It was a pedigree Chinook sled dog, which towed Miss Faulkner's clubs around on a specially made golf cart, but I suspect the interest for readers was not so much that the dog acted as caddie, as that the photograph of his mistress showed a very good-looking young lady wearing short shorts as she addressed the ball. Bruce, a swan which nests at Wildwood GC in Surrey, earns his keep by standing guard outside the pro shop. The course, with its thirteen lakes, provides a home for hundreds of ducks and moorhens as well as Bruce and his mate Sheila (who are not Australian black swans despite their names), and so far most of the golfers have avoided hitting most of the birds most of the time.

Golfers have over the years acquired a reputation for slaughtering wildlife as deadly as any big game hunter of the 1930s. In the 1860s, a Royal & Ancient member even acquired the nickname 'Kill The Cuddy'. While playing at Musselburgh, his drive hit a donkey, or cuddy, and killed it. Nothing more is known about this golfer, except that he used a Robert Forgan club to carry out his deadly mission. In 1993, a farmer in Sweden sued a golf course adjoining her farm, claiming that several of her best cows had died of a 'blocked gaseous transfer' after swallowing golf balls. Large ruminants swallowing golf balls are obviously a major problem in Sweden. At Bjorkliden Arctic Golfklubb, the most northerly course in Europe, there is a local rule which states: 'If a reindeer eats your ball, drop a new one where the incident occurred.'

Possibly the largest animal to affect the lives of golfers is the hippopotamus. At Jinja GC in Uganda, on the northern shores of Lake Victoria, it was reported in April 1943 that a local rule stated: 'On the green a ball lying in a hippo footmark may be lifted and placed not nearer the hole without penalty.' This rule was only applicable, however, when the footprint was at least 18 inches across and two inches deep. To play to your full potential at Jinja, you need more than just a full set of clubs in your bag. You also need a tape measure.

Slightly less vast than a hippo, but more likely to wreak havoc on the golf course, is the horse. During the semi-final of the 1908 Ladies' British Open Amateur Championship at St Andrews, between Maud Titterton and Cecil Leitch, a horse and cart bolted across the course and smashed its cart to smithereens just as Miss Titterton lined up her putt at the Road Hole. Miss Titterton missed her putt as a result, but won the match at the last hole, and went on to win the final against Dorothy Campbell. That was the only time that Miss Titterton won the Ladies' Amateur title, but both Cecil Leitch and Dorothy Campbell went on to win it repeatedly in years to come. Miss Leitch (christened Cecilia but always known as Cecil) held the title from 1914 until 1922, thanks not only to her three successive victories but also to the Great War and a railway strike in 1919, which caused the cancellation of that year's championship.

Dale Bown, playing the 8th hole at Rye during the annual Oxford and Cambridge Golfing Society's President's Putter competition in January 1930, showed far greater composure than Maud Titterton. As Bown lined up his putt, John Morrison, that year's secretary of the Society, rode past the green on the club horse, which he had decided needed some exercise. Bown roared with laughter at the incongruous sight, then gave his 18-yard putt a sharp jab which sent it unerringly to the bottom of the cup. He went on to win his match 3 and 2.

Under the trees near the 18th green at Ham Manor GC, in Angmering, West Sussex, there is a simple headstone, engraved 'Frederick, 1837'. Frederick was a racehorse which won the Derby in 1829, as a 40–1 outsider. A bay colt by Little John out of a mare by Phantom, Frederick was owned by Mr G.W. Gratwicke and trained and ridden by Mr J. Forth. Frederick won the 17-horse race by a head, and earned his owner the astonishing sum of £2,650. Frederick has no real connection with golf, but the Ham Manor club, which was not opened until 99 years after his death, is the only club in Britain to have a Derby winner buried near the 18th green.

In Fairbanks, Alaska, a new course has recently been opened, much to the disgust of a local fox, known to the local golfers as Reynard. Reynard is so upset at having his natural habitat overrun with golfing impedimenta that he is frequently to be seen stealing golf balls from bunkers, from the rough and even from the middle of fairways. Most golfers do not mind a wild beast running off with a ball which has disappeared into a vast sand trap or the impenetrable rough, but it is a gentle soul indeed who can remain calm when a perfectly good drive down the middle of the fairway is stolen by a fox.

106

Dogs have a major part to play on the golf course too. It was Ben Hogan who was reputed to have holed a crucial putt at the same time as a dog was running between his legs. When asked if the animal had put him off, Hogan merely replied, 'What dog?' This story is generally told of the 1954 Masters, but it may well be apocryphal, as a very similar tale is also told of the legendary lady golfer, Joyce Wethered, later Lady Heathcoat Amory, whose concentration on the golf course was total. Horace Hutchinson, the Amateur Champion of 1887, recounts that when playing at Bembridge GC on the Isle of Wight that year, 'I pulled my first tee shot very badly into the harbour. The tide was out, and after a long search over some poisonous mud, we at length found the ball inside a dead and derelict dog. Dead, indeed, but faintly expresses him, he had been dead so long. After this I naturally lost a hole or two.' Most of us would have played three from the tee. Twelve years later *Golfers' Magazine* reported a player in East Anglia who hit his ball into a garden within the reach of a chained up and very alive dog. The hole was abandoned.

Major N.H.D. Pratt, a member at the North Hants GC, at Fleet, used regularly to take his Labrador with him when he played. In March 1960 he wrote to *Golf Illustrated* to say that his drive at the 11th tee struck a crow and killed it. It was fortunate for him, if not for the crow, that ball and bird collided because 'the drive was a badly hit low hook, which was rapidly disappearing in the direction of some low gorse'. His dog retrieved the crow, the crow having by its death retrieved Major Pratt's par.

Our family cat, a large black and white thing called Mouche, was killed by a golf ball on Harpenden Common golf course in 1971. The cat was discovered one afternoon in obvious pain by the third green, just over the road from our house, with a golf ball shaped indentation in its skull. It was taken to the vet who, with great skill and expense, kept the poor cat alive for several days. She finally succumbed, having used up all her lives, leaving only a dent in her skull and in my father's bank balance.

It was reported in May 1993 that Bertha the goose was spending much time in an unavailing attempt to hatch golf balls on her local golf course in Montana. Geese are generally well cared for at golf clubs, but in May 1979, the *Daily Telegraph* reported the strange case of a Canada goose bludgeoned to death with a wooden putter at the 17th hole of the Bethesda Congressional Country Club in Maryland. Dr Sherman Thomas, a 66-year-old member of the club, admitted responsibility, but claimed it was a mercy killing. He said that he had accidentally hit the goose, which lived with its mate on a lake by the green, with his approach shot, and thought that the only humane thing to do was to put it out of its misery with a few well-aimed blows with his putter. However, other evidence seemed to show that the goose had honked as Dr Thomas lined up his putt, and he struck the goose in a rage.

The chairman of the golf committee, Ralph Guglielmi, conducted a hearing, but before the board of governors could take action, Dr Thomas's lawyers (for we are talking about the United States, where lawyers outnumber even golfers) got a court injunction preventing any decision being made while the separate court case was taking place. For this being the United States, the district attorney's office had decided that whether or not the killing was an act of mercy, Dr Thomas had killed a migratory bird out of season (October to January), and what is more he did it with an unapproved weapon, to wit a wooden putter. There was a legal case to answer, in fact two legal cases – the charge of unlawfully killing a migratory bird, and the more serious charge of possessing a goose. The body of the goose had not been seen since Dr Thomas placed it in his golf cart at the scene of the crime.

The final outcome was a bit of plea bargaining. The doctor was found guilty of not possessing a hunting licence, and he was fined $500. But the Bethesda Congressional Club was less merciful. In September that year they suspended him, even though the Canada goose season was about to begin.

Wiping out birds with golf clubs is a routine event. Anne Marie Palli killed a duck with her approach shot to the 9th green during the LPGA Ping/Welch's Championship at Randolph Park, Tucson, Arizona in March 1993. The ball

and the duck both hit the lake after the fatal collision, causing Ms Palli to drop another ball under penalty, and slip to a double bogey 6. Spectacular though her shot was, Councillor Sidney Withers could still teach Anne Marie a few things about slaughtering birds with a golf ball. While playing at Hastings in 1951, Councillor Withers managed to kill two starlings with one shot. 'The birds were flying close together,' he said in mitigation of his horrendous deed. 'My ball struck one and then the other.' As far as can be discovered, nobody has yet killed more than two birds with one golf shot.

If Councillor Withers had played the Zambian Golf Union course at Lusaka, he would have been in all sorts of trouble, despite his high official status. The local rule states clearly that 'peacocks, guinea fowl, duikers, impala etc. have the right of the course. Anyone causing injury or death to any of these birds or animals will suffer the following penalty: immediate and ignominious suspension from the State House golf course'. And, occasionally, birds get their own back on the golfers. On 11 February 1992 at Derby Sinfin Golf Course, Alf Miles drove his second shot at the 16th into a bunker. His dismay was quickly turned to joy when he saw a large crow fly into the bunker and emerge a few seconds later with his ball in its beak. The crow then dropped the ball on the fairway, about ten yards nearer the green. Just as Alf was putting away his sand wedge and getting out his 8-iron, the crow picked up his ball again, and flew off, into a tree adjoining the fairway. Alf and his playing partner Ben Lyle gave chase, but this only encouraged the crow to fly off again, still carrying the ball, until it landed in another tree, near the 13th fairway. The crow then flew off, *sans* ball, leaving Mr Miles with the problem, once so famously and successfully solved by Bernhard Langer, of how to hit his ball out of the tree. He decided not to bother. Score one for the crows.

Score another one for the squirrel that came up against Iain Wallace's golf bag at Scarborough North Cliff GC early in 1993. Wallace walked back to his trolley after holing out on the 8th green to find a squirrel attacking his smart white golf bag. The squirrel's sense of smell had not been weakened by months of hibernation, and it had worked out that there was chocolate there for whoever had the sharpest teeth. Even when Iain put his putter back into the bag, the squirrel was not to be diverted from its mission. Finally, it was bribed to go away with another piece of fruit and nut chocolate, and Wallace's round continued.

Some encounters with wildlife are more serious, and the round cannot continue. Mr Fok Keng Choy had such an encounter. Mr Fok, 43, a former athlete who held the

Singapore national shot putt and discus records in the 1970s, was playing golf at the Tanglin GC in Napier Road, Singapore in August 1993 when he felt the need to pay a visit to the Gents near the course booking office. This was not the best idea he had had all day, for hardly had he locked the door behind him when, according to the *Straits Times*, he was bitten on his testicles by a python which he had not noticed hiding in the toilet bowl he was sitting on. He was bleeding and in pain, but managed to call for help. He was taken to Gleneagles Hospital where he received stitches in his wound. His wife was reported as saying that 'snakes are common here, but not in toilets'. Pest control officers later caught an eight-foot python. The bite of the python is not poisonous, as it normally kills its victims by constricting them. It was lucky for the remarkably unobservant Mr Fok that the python went for the bite rather than the squeeze when presented with such a tempting target.

111

David Feherty, the Irish professional, was bitten by an adder, a biter rather than a squeezer, at Wentworth and his arm swelled to twice its normal size. Feherty's only comment was, 'I wish it had bitten me a bit lower down.' But in general snakes on the course do not bite. In Arizona, there is a course where a local rule reads, 'If your ball lands within a club length of a rattlesnake, you are allowed to move the ball.' The only question is, how? His Excellency Michael John Carlisle (James) Glaze CMG, who lists his recreations in *Who's Who* as golf, grand opera and gardening, managed to combine all three in his battles with snakes on the golf course. When he was HM

Ambassador to the Cameroons between 1984 and 1987, he regularly played at Yaoundé, where snakes were a visible part of the wildlife. On one occasion, a player was addressing his ball on the tee, and had begun his backswing, when a snake slithered through his legs and towards the ball. The golfer, instead of completing his stroke, quite understandably swung his club down on the invading snake, and decapitated it as surely as John the Baptist was decapitated for Salome. The immediate crisis was survived, but a greater one then arose. Had the blow which killed the snake been a 'stroke' as defined by Rule 14: Striking The Ball, and should the killer therefore be deemed to lose a shot? After all, he had dug up quite a divot in slaughtering the snake, which would have offended Mr Glaze's gardening sensitivities. Or even worse, was the ball 'fairly struck at' (Rule 14–1), for the breach of which rule there is a two-stroke penalty? Not even Her Majesty's Ambassador and Plenipotentiary could come up with a satisfactory answer, so it was referred to the R&A Rules of Golf Committee for a ruling. They ruled eventually that the action of 'transforming the snake from an outside agency to a loose impediment' was fully justified under the circumstances, and that therefore he should not be penalized. A happy ending for all but the snake.

Jimmy Stewart, a pro playing in India in 1972, was another golfer who would have had to clean his clubs very thoroughly at the end of the round. As he walked towards his ball to take his second shot from the fairway towards the third hole, he found a ten-foot cobra heading for it as well. He pulled out a suitable club, probably a 1-iron,

112

which has no other discernible use to the average golfer, and killed the snake. Another cobra immediately emerged from the dead cobra's mouth, probably a foot or two shorter but just as deadly, so Stewart, who had not yet put away his 1-iron, killed it as well. No more snakes emerged, and Stewart went on to complete his round.

Probably the smallest item of wildlife that has affected the outcome of a major championship is the insect (species unknown) which cost Lloyd Mangrum the 1950 US Open. Mangrum was in an 18-hole play-off with Ben Hogan and George Fazio at Merion, Pennsylvania, after all three had tied on 287 after four rounds. He was just one stroke behind the great Hogan as he reached the 16th green with a simple putt of six feet or so for his par. He noticed an insect on his ball, so he marked the ball, picked it up and blew the insect off. He then replaced the ball, holed the putt and headed for the 17th. By this time, Fazio was out of contention, but Mangrum believed he could still catch Hogan. But then fate and the rulebook intervened. An official told him that he was penalized two strokes for lifting and cleaning his ball on the green. The sad truth was that although the US Tour rules at the time allowed the lifting and cleaning of balls on the green, the USGA rules which governed the US Open did not. Mangrum was now three behind with two to play. He failed to make up the deficit. Mangrum, whose temperament was perfect for a top golfer, merely commented, 'Well, I guess we'll all still eat tomorrow.'

Fishing and golf go together. It was Julius Boros who said, when asked if he was ever going to retire, 'Me retire?

Retire to what? All I do now is fish and play golf.' Many top golfers are keen fishermen, from Nick Faldo and Greg Norman down. At the East Sussex National GC, at Uckfield, there is a lake stocked with brown trout, where members can fish, and at the Jack Nicklaus designed St Mellion course there is a pond in front of the 5th tee which is also well stocked with trout. The St Mellion course, which hosts the Benson and Hedges International Open rather too early in each year to get the full benefit of Cornwall's climate, has been described by Mark Roe as being designed by the devil. Anders Forsbrand's opinion is more forthright and less printable than Roe's, but St Mellion wins friends as a place to fish if not to play golf.

Animals are a complication on the golf course, from insects to hippos, from snakes to horses, from porcupines like the one at Jasper Park GC, in British Columbia, which regularly creates a thorny problem for any golfer whose ball lands too near, to skylarks like the ones who nested too close to where Doug Sanders' shot landed during a practice round before the 1971 Open at Royal Birkdale. The skylarks' nest, just beyond the 9th green, contained several chicks, but Sanders managed to play on without disturbing them more than they were disturbing him.

If you hit the ball along the ground, it will probably collide with something furry and dangerous. At Karen, in Kenya, there is a sign on the course, advising golfers not to hesitate if a leopard comes out of the bush. It counts as a local rule which trumps Rule 6–8 on Discontinuance of Play. The R&A did not think of leopards when considering reasons why play could legitimately be discontinued. If you hit the ball in the air, it will probably hit a goose or a starling, like the one that diverted P.B. Wilson's ball as it soared majestically towards the 5th green at Howth GC, near Dublin, in 1924, resulting in a quadruple bogey instead of a possible par. And if you hit it in the water, you will probably hit either a trout or a crocodile, or possibly another player retrieving his ball. Whichever one it is, it will do your score no good. The only playable golf course is one without wildlife, but the only course without wildlife so far discovered is the Fra Mauro crater on the moon. And even that has not proved to be very playable.

115

DROPPED SHOTS

Crocodile in lake alongside green
Elephant Hills GC, Zimbabwe

30 artificial crocodiles basking by green
Lost City Resort, Sun City, South Africa

Dogs trained to find golf balls by the smell of their paint
Westward Ho! GC, 1970s

Dung relief given
at L'Ancresse, Guernsey

Cow killed by golf ball
by W.J. Robinson, at St Margaret's-at-Cliffe GC, Kent, 13 June 1934

Flying swallow cut in two by golf ball
at Nahant Links, 1897

Robin killed in flight by golf ball
at Baltusrol GC, 1924

Cock killed by golf ball
at Musselburgh, 1896

Trout killed by golf ball
at Newark, Nottinghamshire, May 1907

Hare killed by golf ball
by Capt. Ferguson at Kilspindie GC, Longniddry, East Lothian, 10 June 1904

Rabbit merely stunned by golf ball
at Gullane GC, East Lothian, 1897

Small bear sniffs ball on fairway
at Jasper Park GC, Canada, ball played by Ralph Kennedy (Winged Foot GC), 1930s

Six long-tailed monkeys wrestling on 8th tee while players driving off
2nd round, South African Open, Durban Country Club, December 1980

Crow steals 30 golf balls
at Lithgow GC, New South Wales, during Easter Tournament, 1972

Ball driven into nest of Vanellus coronatus (crowned plover) without disturbing the eggs
Metropolitan GC, Cape Town, 1951

'Suggest that all the birds living by the second green be given diapers to protect the seat'
Suggestion dated 25 May 1952 in Royal St George's GC suggestion book

'Laundry charges prohibit this admirable suggestion'
Official committee response

LIES, DAMNED LIES ![7]

AND STATISTICS

R alph A. Kennedy was born on 16 June 1882, but was not introduced to golf until 1910, when he was 28 years old. In 1919 he read the claim of one Charles Fletcher, an English actor who was obviously a man who specialized in resting between engagements, who was said to have played golf on a world record total of 240 different golf courses. Mr Kennedy decided that this was a record asking to be beaten and, pausing only to become a founder member of Winged Foot GC in Mamaroneck, New York State in 1921, he set about playing golf wherever he could. It was early in the 1920s that he claimed the record, but he decided not to stop there. On one day, 22 February

1931, he played rounds in four different states, and on his fiftieth birthday, in 1932, he played Timber Point GC, on Long Island, which became the 1,000th course in his collection. Eight years later he brought his total up to 2,000. His 2,500th course was Pebble Beach, Monterey, California in 1946 and his 3,000th was St Andrews on 17 September 1951, where he shot a 93. By this time he was playing an average of two new courses every week of the year, at the age of almost seventy. During his 24-day trip to Britain to play St Andrews as his 3,000th course, he played 35 new courses: 26 in Scotland, seven in England and two in Ireland. His final tally before he went to the Great Clubhouse in the Sky is uncertain, but it was well on the way to 4,000. He reckoned to have played around half the golf courses that existed in the United States in 1950, as well as over 400 in Canada, twenty in South America, and others in Bermuda, Cuba, Mexico and Europe.

During this endless voyage over significantly more than 50,000 different holes, Ralph Kennedy managed to hole only four of his tee shots. Two of these shots were genuine aces, one was a three because his first shot from the tee had landed in the water, but his most bizarre counted as a four. He was playing Maple GC, in Rhode Island, and used a 4-wood at the 170-yard 9th hole. The ball soared over a large maple tree which stood between the tee and the green, and wedged in the side of the hole, but not all below the rim of the cup. What his playing partner was prepared to concede was a hole-in-one was deemed by Mr Kennedy to be an unplayable lie. The ball was removed, with a two-stroke penalty, and then putted back into the cup. This time it fell to the very bottom, giving Kennedy a 4 for his hole-in-one. He sent a description of the event to the USGA, who upheld his view. 'I liked that 4 better than a hole-in-one,' said the ever cheerful Mr Kennedy.

Ralph Kennedy's success in holing only four tee shots out of 50,000 implies that there is no better than a 12,500 to 1 chance of making a hole-in-one. However, the odds against a hole-in-one for a professional male golfer, as quoted in the *Golfer's Handbook*, are a more achievable 3,708 to 1, while for the average golfer they lengthen to 42,952 to 1. Mr Kennedy was obviously quite good in his prime.

Holes-in-one are no longer a curiosity, a fact that was noted with regret in 1927. Up until then there had been a Hole In One Club, based in Newark, Ohio. In its first years of existence, everybody who managed an ace was given a dozen golf balls. This became rather expensive for the sponsors, who decided a badge would be an acceptable and cheaper substitute. But by March 1927, even supplying badges was uneconomical for the club, and it was disbanded. A brief announcement stated that it had been discontinued 'owing to the frequency with which aces have been accomplished during the past few years'. By 1927, the club had over 10,000 members, making it the only golf club in the history of the game that has had to close because it was growing too quickly.

These days it is even possible to insure against a hole-in-one. Art Wall Jr, the American golfer who won the 1959 Masters, had by that year scored 35 aces, beginning at the age of 12 in 1935, at his home course of Honesdale, Pa. By 1959, he had taken out an insurance policy with Lloyd's of London, which, for a $4 annual premium, paid him $400 every time he added to his amazing total of holes-in-one. He ended up with 42 of them, but remains second in the all-time list to Norman Manley of Long Beach, California, who has 47 to his credit and thus holds the title either of the World's Luckiest Golfer or the World's Most Believable Liar.

120

Guardian Royal Exchange runs a policy which throws in free cover against the cost of celebrating a hole-in-one if you insure your golf clubs against theft, but it did not cover the unfortunate golfer in New Zealand who in 1994 shot a hole-in-one and dropped dead a couple of hours later. Hole-in-one insurance got off to a rocky start in Australia, according to a *Daily Telegraph* report in May 1976, when one particular club asked for a policy to insure itself against having to pay out the prize money it gave for holes-in-one. The club committee, realizing that it would do the club a lot of good if a lot of people won the prize, shaped the green on one of the shorter holes like a saucer, so that tee shots landing on the green were inclined to slide gently down the slope and into the hole. For a short while everybody at the club was pleased with the way the insurance policy was working. The players who achieved a hole-in-one were winning big money prizes, and the committee was not having to dig into its own coffers to award the prizes. But it did not take the insurers long to work out what was happening. 'After that,' said a Lloyd's spokesman, 'we made sure that this type of

risk was only accepted in recognized tournaments and on approved courses.'

Some holes-in-one still merit the title of curiosity: a hole-in-one caused by an earthquake, for example. *Golf Illustrated* reported that, in May 1932, a golfer was playing at 10 a.m. in Mexico City when an earthquake struck. He had driven his ball on to the 9th green, and it had stopped at the very edge of the hole. As he stepped forward to putt it in for a two, the earthquake struck, and his ball fell into the hole.

Holes-in-one are obviously not things you can practise for, especially if an earthquake gets in the way. Gary Player's famous maxim that 'the more I practise, the luckier I get' does not seem to apply to aces, as Player has not accrued more than his fair share. In fact, Dennis Kemp of Abbotskerswell seems to prove that the less you practise, the luckier you get. At the age of 82, Mr Kemp, who was following a game being played by his son at Reigate Heath, Surrey, decided to borrow a club and have a swing at the

158-yard 15th hole. This was his first swing of a golf club for 15 years, and despite being blind in one eye (like Tommy Armour), Mr Kemp holed his tee shot. In July 1932 Edward J. Morrison, another man to whom golfing consistency is a stranger, was playing the 108-yard 17th hole at Rye Country Club. His tee shot hit a house 50 yards beyond the green, and bounced back into the cup.

Not everybody would describe a hole-in-one as their dreams come true. In Japan, the cost of a hole-in-one is astronomical. It's not just a case of buying drinks for all and sundry at the 19th hole. In Japan, you are expected to pay for expensive mementos for your playing partners, not to mention a large official drinks party and the planting of a commemorative tree near what is rather doubtfully called, in best Japlish, the 'joy spot'. As the 'joy spot' is inevitably either where the shot began on the tee or where it ended on the green, and as it is not permitted even in Japan to plant trees on the green, this means that, in a few years, we can expect most tees on most par-3 holes in Japan to be in the middle of a rapidly burgeoning forest of celebratory trees. Playing out of a wood will at least have the effect of reducing the number of holes-in-one in future.

The nearest to a hole-in-one without actually being able to claim it is a record shared by Dr E.R.S. Grice and Mr L. Watson. They were playing in the first round of the Walsall Golf Club's Newport Cup competition, and both made strong drives at the 182-yard 4th hole. Both balls were obviously on the green, but the hole itself was hidden by bunkers. When they reached the green, they found that one ball was visible, a short distance from the pin. The other ball was in the hole. Both players had taken a new ball at the hole, and now both turned out to be using the same make and number of ball, so it was completely impossible to tell which player had scored the ace. The only thing for it was for the two men to return to the 4th tee and play again. This they did, but neither holed out at the second attempt.

John C. Stuart holed the 135-yard 13th hole at Carnoustie in March 1950, at the age of 78. This was the second ace of his career, the previous one having been sixty years earlier. Whether this is the longest gap ever recorded between holes-in-one is not known, but it is very likely to be the only case of a golfer scoring 50 per cent of his holes-in-one left-handed and 50 per cent right-handed. Mr Stuart took up golf as a left-hander, and scored his 1890 ace left-handed. Three years later, he changed to a right-handed stance, and he was still playing right-handed when he holed the 13th at Carnoustie in 1950.

Golf is a rarity among ball games, in that left-handers do not flourish. In cricket, for example, there are Garfield Sobers, David Gower and Frank Woolley, and in tennis Rod Laver, John McEnroe and Martina Navratilova. In baseball there have been Babe Ruth and Sandy Koufax, not to mention Lefty Grove or the switch-hitting Mickey Mantle, and in boxing there have been many world champion southpaws. But in golf there are almost no great left-handers. The great Harry Vardon remarked that he 'never saw one worth a damn'. Bob Charles of New Zealand remains the only left-hander to have won the Open, his

123

year being 1963, and by 1993, he was the all-time leading money-winner on the US Senior Tour. P.B. 'Laddie' Lucas is the only left-hander to have captained the British Walker Cup team, which he did in 1949. In recent years only Phil Mickelson, who won the 1991 Tucson Open as an amateur, has shown that playing left-handed is no bar to playing at the very top level.

The Left Handers Golf Association of America was formed in June 1932, with Babe Ruth as its first President, but the odd thing is that many people who play golf left-handed are not naturally left-handed at all. Bob Charles is right-handed, while Johnny Miller and Curtis Strange, who both play golf right-handed, are naturally left-handed. The late Sewsunker Sewgolum, the South African professional who won the Dutch Open from time to time, played right-handed but with his left hand lower down the club than his right hand – the wrong way round. It all comes down to how you are taught. *Golf Magazine* reported in February 1894 that 'at Grantown, the fashionable resort on the Spey, where golf was introduced by a left-handed player, nearly everyone uses the left hand to play. A visitor to the place lately found that it was difficult to get a right-handed club.'

Those were the days when all you needed was one club, whether left-handed or right-handed, but these days it is a curiosity to find people playing a complete round with just one club. Gloria Minoprio, a member of the Littlestone Golf Club in Kent, caused a front-page sensation by turning up for the first round of the English Ladies' Championship of 1933 at the Royal North Devon GC at Westward Ho! with only one club, a long-shafted iron which these days would be classified as either a 1-iron or a 2-iron. Her caddie held a spare club and a spare ball. She was playing Miss Nancy Halstead in the first round, and eventually lost 5 and 3. Miss Halstead, using a full set of clubs, went on to the semi-final round of the Championship. What caused the sensation, though, was not Miss Minoprio's bizarre preference for just one club, and the most difficult one in the bag at that, but the fact that she turned up to play wearing a neat woollen navy beret, a turtle-necked sweater and – horror of horrors – navy slacks. It did not matter that the trousers were of the most elegant cut or that she was without doubt the most elegant of all the competitors. Trousers had never been worn before by a woman in an important championship, or indeed probably ever on any golf course in Britain. The Chairman of the Ladies' Golf Union issued a brief statement saying that she regretted 'this departure from the usual golfing costume at the Championship'. However, Miss Minoprio came back to play in the Championship over the next two years, still wearing slacks and still using just one club.

In 1934, Miss Minoprio won her first-round match, against Betty Sommerville, by 2 and 1, but went out in the second round. In 1935, the weather at Royal Birkdale was so vile that many of the competitors wore waterproof trousers, but none except Gloria Minoprio used just one club. She had a bye in the first round, a walkover in the second, but in the third round she was beaten, 4 and 2 by Audrey Holmes of Essex. In 1936, at the British Ladies' Championship, she lost again in the first round, but at least she qualified, her one-club qualifying rounds being a 90 and an 84. In the spring of 1938, she beat Miss Wain Winter of South Africa at the British Championship by a margin of 4 and 3. Miss Winter thus became probably the last person ever beaten in an important event by somebody playing with only one club throughout. It was no humiliation, however, for Miss Minoprio had been practising over the Championship course, at Burnham and Berrow in Somerset, for weeks and had shot a 79, which would not be too bad for somebody carrying a complete bag full of clubs. When Charles Hutchings went round Royal Liverpool GC at the turn of the century in 81, using just a 'long-shafted putting cleek', it was deemed to be a major achievement, so there can be no doubt that Gloria Minoprio was a fine if eccentric golfer.

However many clubs you set out with, sometimes the ball will contrive to land in such a place that none of the set will be of much help. Bernhard Langer is not the only player to have played from high up in the foliage in a

major championship. Ben Sayers, who is now remembered mainly as a clubmaker but was reputed to have played in every Open from 1880 to 1923, was only five feet three inches tall and in his youth had been a professional acrobat. When he hit his ball into the ivy near the roof of Wemyss Castle during a professional tournament at the end of the last century, he simply scrambled up the side of the wall 'like a squirrel', according to contemporary reports, and played a fine recovery shot from his unusual lie.

Balls have landed in bottles (most famously, the ball of Irishman Harry Bradshaw in the 1949 Open at Royal St George's; in binocular cases (as happened to Tony Jacklin's ball in the third round of the 1971 Open at Royal Birkdale); and on a set of false teeth. Mrs S. Lloyd was playing in Cheshire in 1981 when her ball landed on a complete upper set of dentures. She considered them a loose impediment and put them in her pocket. At the end of the round she gave them to the pro, who told her that if they were not claimed in three weeks, they were hers. Balls also land regularly on the clubhouse roof. During the Varsity match of 1904, played at Woking, Mr Allison of Oxford took what was described as the direct route to the 18th green, by hitting his ball on to the clubhouse roof. Most players would have dropped another ball, but Mr Allison was made of sterner stuff. He climbed up a ladder on to the roof, which was fortunately flat, and then played his approach shot from the roof to the green, with pinpoint accuracy. By the time Mr Allison had climbed back down to ground level, his pockets were bulging with lost balls, which he sold to his fellow players at a very reasonable price after lunch.

Mr Allison was neither the first nor the last to treat houses as loose impediments. Phil Bozzuto played a shot from the top of a shed during the Palm Desert Classic in 1960. He got a bogey 4. Nicol Thompson Jr of Canada was playing the final hole of a tournament at Belmont Manor GC in Bermuda on 2 March 1932, and heading towards what looked like a certain victory when he hit his ball on to a hotel roof. The dropped shots caused by this wild hook meant that the tournament went to play-off, which Thompson lost. At Pennant Hills GC, Sydney, in 1951, club member Ken Duncan sliced his drive at the 3rd tee. The ball shot off in an out-of-bounds direction and bounced on the tiled roof of a house. Duncan went off to look for his ball, to be met by the lady of the house. She was holding a rather dirty ball in her hand. It had fallen down the chimney. At least Ken Duncan was able to make his way back to the course after his foray into the outside world: Roberto de Vicenzo was less lucky during the 1965

World Cup in Madrid. He hooked his ball out of bounds, and an over-zealous official refused to let him back on to the course after he had retrieved his ball. He had to buy a ticket to get back in bounds.

The clubhouse is not always out of bounds, though. When Nigel Denham played his second shot to the 18th a little too strongly during the English Open Amateur Strokeplay Championship at Moortown GC Leeds, in 1974, the ball bounced up the clubhouse steps and pinged off a wall and into the bar. Playing the 19th hole before completing the 18th is unusual, but Denham did not hesitate. He opened a window and pitched the ball back on to the green to within ten feet of the cup. The R&A subsequently ruled that Denham should have been penalized two strokes for opening the window, on the principle that the clubhouse was an immovable object and that therefore no part of it should have been moved. As an amateur, Denham obviously felt that the bill for a new pane of glass was more financially debilitating than the risk of not winning the Championship.

The Golf Nut Society Of America reported in 1994 that a member has a regular habit of opening the glass door of his apartment and hitting practice drives through the opening. On one occasion, he pulled his shot and it hit the door frame at full power. The ball ricocheted back past his head and embedded itself in the wall behind him. The golfer has left the ball there as a reminder to hit straighter in future. M. Bull, playing the Meyrick Park course in Bournemouth in August 1915, had less luck with his ricochet. He was playing out of a wood at the 16th hole when his ball hit a tree and rebounded into his golf bag, which was being held by his caddie who was standing ten yards behind him.

Bobby Jones used the ricochet to great effect in the 1921 Amateur Championship at Hoylake, the first tournament he ever played in Britain. At the 8th hole in his fourth-round match against the eventual finalist Allan Graham, he found himself with a near impossible lie next to a fence to the left of the green. Rather than play it in the direction of the green with an almost entirely restricted backswing, Jones chose to play the ball with a full flowing stroke straight at the palings. It rebounded as planned on to the green.

130

At Bray in Co. Wicklow, in 1910, a Dublin cyclist, Mr W. Lee, was riding his bike away from the clubhouse when a player driving from the 8th tee sliced his ball. The slice was so wild but so powerful that the ball jammed between the spokes of the back wheel of Mr Lee's bicycle. Mr Lee, being a keen cyclist rather than a keen golfer, was unaware of the collision and pedalled off into the distance. He was called back before he finally disappeared out of earshot, and the ball, rather the worse for wear, was retrieved from between the spokes. As *Golf Monthly* reported at the time, 'There is a controversy going on at Bray just now as to what Rule of golf governs such an incident.'

The Irish feature in many of the odder shots of golfing history. In the 1920s, Mr F. A. Wright played a shot at Baltusrol GC, New Jersey, into the hair of an Irish maid. She obviously had a very fine head of hair, because she did not feel the impact, but obligingly walked up the

fairway towards the green, with the ball still in her hair.
A similar but less Irish incident had occurred thirty years
earlier when two players were involved in a match at the
Shelter Island links, on Long Island, New York State, in
1897. The two golfers involved had to turn to George
Strath, the professional at the Wee Burn GC, for a ruling,
because there was a large bet resting on the outcome of
the match. The first golfer, one up with three to play, had
hit his drive into the brim of a woman's hat, without the
woman being aware of it. The erring golfer wanted to
rush after her and get her to drop the ball, but his
opponent, who needed to square the match, insisted that
the ball had lodged in a hazard and must be played from
where it lay, or the hole would be forfeited. He suggested
that the wild driver should stand on the woman's shoulders
to play the ball out of the hat, but the driver reckoned
that if the hat was a hazard, he had the right to ask the
woman to remove it. The eventual judgement, by Strath,
was that the ball had lodged in an unplayable place and

131

that the striker should drop another ball, losing stroke and distance. It is not recorded who eventually won the match.

Several astonishing shots have been played to win major championships, perhaps none more extraordinary than Bobby Jones's drive from the 9th tee during the third round of the US Open in his Grand Slam year, 1930. The drive was by a pond, or over it if you fancied your chances of reaching the green on this par-5 hole in two. Jones went for the big hit, but was distracted in his backswing by two little girls who chose that moment to run across the fairway. The result was a low drive which skidded across the surface of the pond like a bouncing bomb, and landed on the other side, just short of the green. He duly got his birdie. Wayne Westner took a similar route during the third round of the Murphy's English Open at the Forest of Arden GC, on 21 August 1993. His ball landed on an island in the middle of a lake, so Westner removed his trousers, put on his waterproofs, and waded out to the island. He parred the hole, but failed to finish among the leaders.

Trick shots have been developed by many golfers, including Mathias Gronberg of Sweden, who can drop the ball from his mouth as he takes a full swing, and hit the ball before it hits the ground. He never misses. But to be able to make a trick shot work during a championship is rather more difficult. When Jerome D. Travers was playing Oswald Kirkby in the final of the New Jersey Amateur Championship at Baltusrol, he topped his tee shot at the 220-yard 13th hole into a ditch which had become a mudbath thanks to all-day rain. Still, the ball had to be played. He selected a niblick, the equivalent of a modern 9-iron, and hit the ball from mid-air as he was jumping the ditch. He hit the ball out of the bog and strongly in the direction of the hole, to get down in four, one over par. Oswald Kirkby, who drove on to the green, three-putted for a half.

Freddie Tait, the great Scottish golfer, was in the final of the Amateur Championship at Prestwick in 1899, defending his title against John Ball, when he hit his ball into a flooded bunker. The ball floated on the water, but that did not stop Tait from hitting a magnificent recovery shot on to the green. He lost his title to Ball at the 37th hole and within the year he was dead, killed by a Boer sniper at Koodoosberg Drift on 7 February 1900.

133

Balls collide from time to time, as Harold Hilton confirmed in *Golf Illustrated* in 1916: 'I myself have seen it happen more than once. I know of one case when one of the balls was holed out after coming in contact with the opponent's ball.' At the turn of the century, Willie Park played Harry Vardon for £100, and they halved the first ten holes. On the 11th hole, Vardon, driving second, hit Park's ball as it pitched. The balls did not fly off in odd directions as a result of this collision, but the effect on Park was devastating. He was so unnerved by the length of Vardon's drive that his game fell away, and Vardon won every hole thereafter.

The precision of Vardon's game was legendary. In 1900, he was on a protracted exhibition tour of America, during which he made a personal appearance at the Boston department store, Jordan Marsh. Hitting balls into a net all day was not his idea of excitement, so he brightened up his life by aiming at the handle of a fire extinguisher that was sticking through the netting. The handle was scarcely bigger than a coin, but Vardon was able to hit it so often that the manager had to ask him to stop, for fear of flooding the store. Vardon is probably the only golfer to have created by his accuracy a water hazard inside an immovable object.

134

DROPPED SHOTS

Lost on play-offs for all four major titles
Craig Wood, USA (Open 1933; US PGA 1934; Masters 1935; US Open 1939)
Greg Norman, Australia (US Open 1984; Masters 1987; Open 1989; US PGA 1993)

Three major titles in one year
Ben Hogan (US), 1953. Hogan did not compete in the fourth major, the US PGA, that year. He only ever competed in the Open in 1953

All four major titles at least once in a career
Gene Sarazen (US), by 1935; Ben Hogan (US) by 1953; Gary Player (South Africa) by 1965; and Jack Nicklaus (US) by 1966

All four major titles at least three times each in a career
Jack Nicklaus (US) by 1978

Eleven consecutive professional tournament victories
Byron Nelson (US), in 1945

Thirteen South African Open victories
Gary Player (South Africa), to 1981

Nine New Zealand Open victories
Peter Thomson (Australia), to 1971

Nine Irish National Professional titles
Christy O'Connor (Ireland), to 1978

Fifteen Northumberland Ladies' Amateur Championship titles in 27 years
Mrs Margaret Pickard (née Nichol), between 1956 and 1982

Eleven Canadian Ladies' Open Amateur Championship titles
Marlene Stewart, between 1951 and 1973

Drive of 2,640 yards across ice
Nils Lied, at Mawson Base, Antarctica, 1962

Drive of 787 yards at a 456-yard hole
Carl Hooper, at the 3rd hole, Oak Hills Country Club, during the Texas Open Championship, 1992

Drive of 634 yards 4 inches
Liam Higgins at Baldonnel military airport, Dublin, 25 September 1984.

Drive of 515 yards
Michael Austin, at the 5th hole, Winterwood GC, Las Vegas, Nevada, US National Seniors Championship, 25 September 1974

Drive of 500 yards
George Bayer, in Australia, 1950s, backed by a strong wind

Drive of 483 yards
F. Lemarchand, at the 13th hole, Westward Ho! GC, backed by a gale

Drive of 450 yards
T.H.V. Haydon, at the 9th hole, East Devon GC, Budleigh Salterton, September 1934

Drive of 445 yards
Edward C. Bliss at the 9th hole, Old Course, Herne Bay GC, August 1913

Drive of 435 yards 3 inches
Brian Pavlet of Phoenix, Arizona, at US National Long-Driving competition, Utah, 1993

Drive of 430 yards
Craig Wood, at the 530-yard 5th hole at the Old Course, St Andrews, in the Open Championship, June 1933

135

Drive of 353 yards from the Savoy Hotel roof into the Thames
Tony Jacklin, 26 November 1969

Drive from the Savoy Hotel roof to the other side of the Thames
Walter Hagen, 1928

Green on 493-yard hole reached in two by a woman
Laura Davies at the USLPGA Open, 1987, Plainview, New Jersey

Drive of 200 yards horizontally and 2 miles vertically
Arthur Lynskey, from the top of Pikes Peak, Colorado, 28 June 1968

Ball struck 250 yards from tee on to gang mower, which then drove down the fairway and back to the tee
Robin Quantrill, at Shillinglee Park, Surrey, 1992

11 birdies in one round
J-M Canizares (Spain) at Crans-sur-Sierre, Switzerland

Round of 233 (163 over par)
'A junior member' of Peterhead Golf Club in atrocious weather conditions at Aberdeen Links, 1974

Round of 172 (100 over par)
Ken Venturi, aged 12, 1943 (his first round)

Round of 121 at the Open
Maurice Flitcroft, during qualifying at Formby, 1976

Round of 83 using only a putter
Joe Kirkwood, at Bellair GC, USA, playing with Babe Ruth and Gene Sarazen on 2 March 1932

13 at 155-yard hole in major championship
Tom Watson at the 12th hole in the 1980 Masters

Hole-in-one in the Ryder Cup
Peter Butler (UK) at the 16th hole at Muirfield, 1973
Nick Faldo (Europe) at the 14th hole at the Belfry, 1993

Hole-in-one by an Open Champion on way to victory
James Anderson (Scotland), at the 17th hole at St Andrews, 1878
Jock Hutchison (US), at the 145 the yard 8th hole at St Andrews, 1921

Appropriately named hole-in-one
Richard Ace, 6th hole, Gulf Gate GC, Florida, 1993

Hole-in-one for opponent
C. Shaw, at Riverside, California, February 1938

Three holes-in-one in one round
Dr Joseph O. Boydstone, 3rd, 4th and 9th holes at Bakersfield GC, California, 10 October 1962
Revd Harold Snider, 8th, 13th and 14th holes at Ironwood, Arizona, 9 June 1976

Three holes-in-one on successive days at the same hole
Bob Taylor, at the 188-yard 16th hole at Hunstanton GC, Norfolk, 1974

Three holes-in-one at the same hole in successive rounds over four days
18 handicap golfer Mrs Paddy Martin, at the 125-yard 3rd hole at Rickmansworth GC, Hertfordshire, on Good Friday, Easter Saturday and Easter Monday, 1960. In each case she used an 8-iron.

Two holes-in-one in succession
Alex Duthie, 3rd and 4th holes at Vancouver Golf and Country Club, 1920s
Roger Game, 7th and 8th holes at Walmer & Kingsdown GC, Kent, 6 February 1964
Norman L. Manley, 7th and 8th holes at Del Valle Country Club, Saugus, Ca., 2 September 1964. Both these holes were par-4
John Hudson, 11th and 12th holes at Royal Norwich, Norfolk, 1971
Tom Doty, 5th and 6th holes, Chicago, Illinois, October 1971
Sue Prell, 13th and 14th holes, Chatswood GC, Sydney, 29 May 1977

Two holes-in-one at the same hole on the same day
P.H. Morton, 1899
R. Boeckman, at St Cloud Country Club, Minnesota, 22 September 1936
Allan Gibson, at Kirriemuir GC, Angus, 1993

Hole-in-one by husband and wife during respective years as captain
Mr and Mrs H. Jones of Westhoughton GC. Mr Jones aced the 147-yard 3rd hole as captain in 1948; Mrs Jones the 143-yard 1st hole as captain in 1950

Holes-in-one at the same hole by husband and wife
at the 145-yard 9th hole of Iizuka RKB Golf Club, Fukuoka, Japan, by Hideaki Nishio on 1 December 1986 and by his wife Kimiyo on 24 December 1986

Holes-in-one at the same hole by playing partners
C.H. Calhoun and his son, Washington GC, USA, 27 August 1932
W. Harman and M. Godby, at Wellington, New Zealand, 31 May 1936
Two players at Shirley GC New Zealand, 18 July 1936
M. Ikawa and N. Ando, at Gifu, Japan, 26 May 1984

Hole-in-one with first shot with new club
H.A. Cotton, at the 160-yard 15th hole at Robin Hood GC 2 December 1935. The club was a 3-iron

Hole-in-one with only shot ever made in golf
Unnamed Greek man, at the 135-yard 8th hole on pitch and putt course at Edgwarebury, Herts, 1978

Golf ball bounced off pitching wedge 5,172 times
Bob McGregor (Canada) 1993

Right-handed but plays wedge shots left-handed
Massimo Scarpa (Italy), European Amateur Champion 1992

Right-handed but carried a left-handed mashie for when fences or trees interfered with normal stance
Harry Vardon (UK)

Results of statistical surveys
98% of golfers believe golf relieves stress
83% of German golfers take lessons from the course pro
80% of golfers believe golf is a good way to make new business contacts
77% of golfers believe women should be treated equally at golf clubs

75% of Scots men take their wives with them on golfing
holidays
74% of southern Englishmen take their wives with them on
golfing holidays
67% of northern Englishmen leave their wives behind when
taking golfing holidays
55% of golfers daydream about golf during boring business
meetings
50% of British golfers have a handicap of 18 or below
24% of British golfers choose the Algarve for an overseas
golfing holiday
18% of women admit to losing their tempers on a golf course
12% of all golfers say golf is more important than sex
for women, the lower the golf handicap, the higher the salary
earned
the average American male golfing handicap is 16.2
total European Tour winnings average out at £14 for every
golfer in Europe

THE COURSE OF

TRUE LOVE, AND

OTHER THINGS

To most golfers William Gates III was just a 37-year-old 'Super Nerd' who founded the Microsoft computer software corporation and was worth seven billion dollars or so. But when he decided to get married, he showed that he was not all boring. His marriage to Melinda French on New Year's Day 1994 took place on the 17th hole of the Manele Bay golf course, on the southern coast of the Hawaiian island of Lanai. One of his guests was Katharine Graham, the publisher of the *Washington Post* during its Watergate heyday, who was quoted as saying, 'They want a private, human wedding. They don't want publicity.' If they had married on the 18th green, just by the clubhouse, they might have been nearer the reception, but it would not have been as private. It has to be the 17th for privacy.

The pursuit of love and marriage on the golf course is not limited to Hawaii. The actress Glynis Johns said that the film producer Anthony Darnborough proposed to her while they were playing at Sunningdale in 1951. Although Miss Johns accepted the proposal, they never married. Darren Allard of the East Grinstead contract bricklaying company Hall and Coaker was top scorer for his company in their victory in the final of the Times Corporate Golf Challenge, held at the Hyatt La Manga Resort course in Spain in November 1993. As they sealed their victory on the final green, Allard proposed to his girlfriend, Sally Hood, who accepted.

Many men would state unashamedly that Gates, Darnborough and Allard had found the best way to make use of a woman on a golf course, by lining one up as a bride just before the end of the round. Although competitions for women have been a part of every club's routine since the first recorded competition for women was announced by the Musselburgh Golf Club in 1810, many golf clubs are still the last resort of the male chauvinist. The story of the club which had a notice on its door stating 'Dogs and Women Not Allowed' is not apocryphal, although it certainly does not apply to the Honourable Company of Edinburgh Golfers at Muirfield, where dogs are welcome but women are not. The story is told of

141

Elspeth Mustard, secretary to the Secretary at Muirfield, who had to prevent an American lady from entering the clubhouse. 'I am sorry,' said Mrs Mustard from inside the clubhouse, 'we don't allow ladies in the clubhouse.' The American woman could only look carefully at Mrs Mustard and ask, 'Then what are you?' Yet even in America there is segregation of the sexes on the golf course. *Golf Illustrated* in January 1923 proudly announced the opening of America's first women's golf course, the Women's National Golf and Tennis Club at Glenhead, Long Island. Its architect was a man, of course.

142

It would be wrong to assume that golfers dislike women. Walter Hagen married several of them, and Ray Floyd is certainly the only Ryder Cup captain who has managed a topless all-girl band. The Ladybirds, his protégées in the 1960s, failed to earn him as much money as his victories in four majors, but he has never been one to do things just for their financial reward. All the same, golf has been seen as one of the last bastions of masculine privacy, with perhaps twenty times as many men playing the game as women. There is no obvious reason for this, except possibly that late nineteenth-century male clubbishness found its natural format in the shape of a sports club which does not require its members to be good at the sport, or even particularly healthy – the golf club. Then again there is the land required for the golf course. In many cases this was originally owned by a male landowner. The club naturally became a male one, and once the precedent was set, it became very hard to break.

By the 1990s, the walls of masculine domination were

crumbling. In 1993 West Kent GC found its bar licence revoked by local magistrates – unless voting rights were extended to its female members. The club tried to hold out, by living on soft drinks at the 19th hole for a full month, but in the end alcohol proved a stronger motivator than sexism. An extraordinary general meeting was called in May 1993, at which the proposal to extend voting rights to more categories of members, including, for the first time, women members, was carried with scarcely a protest. The chairman, Ron Anthony, said that women members had never complained about the issue, which was never discussed until the magistrates' ruling. 'It has never been a feminist, sexist issue,' he said. 'We have just been doing what most golf clubs have traditionally done, and still do.' The West Kent club increased its voting membership by around 250, from 400 to 650, including just over 100 women, who thus earned equality of voting rights with their male counterparts. However, there was no change in playing rights, and no change in subscription rates, which remain lower for women playing members to reflect their lesser playing privileges. 'Playing rights were never an issue,' said club Secretary Alex Messing, whatever the national press may have felt. Yet playing rights for women across the country are significantly worse than for men. When, in the Channel Four documentary about Northwood GC, shown in 1994, a club member stated that he did not understand how women could have time to play on a Sunday morning because they would have to be busy preparing lunch, he was expressing a view which is still widely held, in Middlesex and elsewhere. When

Joan Askham, women's captain at Grimsby GC, played her home course on a Sunday morning in 1993, she was the first lady ever to do so in the seventy-year history of the club. Whether she still had time to get home and prepare her husband's lunch is not recorded.

By the end of the year, the first woman to be appointed chairman of a golf club had taken office. Mrs Jill Trudgill, a 20 handicap player, took on the role of chairman at the Beadlow Manor Hotel Golf and Country Club in Bedfordshire, having been voted into office by the club's 700 members, of whom around 100 are women. Ten years earlier, women were not even allowed into the clubhouse. If they were hungry or thirsty, they had to eat their sandwiches and drink their coffee in the changing-rooms, a situation which still prevails in many other clubs in Britain.

But if they are in love, they can rely on Arnold Palmer. The great man was booked into the Clifton Arms at Lytham by the organizers of the British Senior Open at Royal Lytham and St Annes, from 22 to 25 July 1993. For reasons best known to the organizers, Palmer was allocated the bridal suite with the four-poster bed, which caused major difficulties for Hans Bolton and his fiancée, Sally Anne Murphy. Hans and Sally were getting married on the Saturday of the tournament, 24 July, and had booked the bridal suite for themselves almost a year in advance. When the hotel told them that the room had been reserved for Mr Palmer, Hans wrote to him hoping, by a perfect combination of flattery and more flattery, to persuade him to give up the suite for the newly-wed Mr and Mrs Bolton. It was not until the day before the wedding that they learned that the letter had worked and Arnie was happy to give up his four-poster for the night, making their wedding day complete. Palmer met the happy couple, gave them a signed photograph and in return was invited to the wedding party in the hotel that night. There he even danced with Sally, despite the fact that neither she nor her husband is a golfer. This is the only known case of a multiple major winner evacuating his hotel room for the sake of true love.

145

The natural result of love and marriage tends to be children. Golfers have families just as frequently as the rest of the population, and sometimes the children inherit the golfing genes of their parents. The theory of natural selection, first elucidated by Charles Darwin, has particular relevance to golf as Darwin's grandson, Bernard, was a fine amateur golfer who played at international level for twenty years and became at the same time probably the greatest of all writers on golf. He played in the first Walker Cup match in 1922 only because one of the originally selected team members, Robert Harris, fell ill. Darwin, who was in America to cover the Cup for *The Times*, was drafted in to play and to be captain as well. He beat the former US Amateur Champion William Fownes, but Britain still went down by eight matches to four.

Golfing families have been strong since the first drives from the first tees in Scotland. The Morrises, father and son, both won the Open in its early years; the twin brothers Willie and Jamie Dunn were major forces in golf from the middle of the nineteenth century, and Willie's son, also Willie, won the first United States Open in 1894.

The Park brothers, Willie and Mungo, both won the Open Championship, as did Willie's son, Willie Jr. In the first 54 years of the Open, up to the First World War, only 22 families ever held the title, of whom nine held the title for a total of 41 years between them. Other leading golf families include the Wethereds, Roger and his sister Joyce (Lady Heathcoat Amory); the Whitcombe brothers, Charles, Ernest and Reg, who all played for Britain in the Ryder Cup; Percy Alliss and his son Peter; the Christy O'Connors, uncle and nephew; and the Scotts, Lady Margaret and her brother the Hon. Michael. Lady Margaret Scott won the Ladies' British Open Amateur Championship in the first three years of its existence, from 1893 to 1895. Her younger brother Michael won the male equivalent forty years later, in 1933, when well into his fifties.

Three married couples have played in the Walker and Curtis Cups for Britain. Michael Bonallack played in nine Walker Cup sides, twice as captain, while his wife Angela played in six Curtis Cup teams. Michael's sister Sally also played in the Curtis Cup in 1962. Ian Caldwell played in two Walker Cup teams in the 1950s, and his wife Carole played in two Curtis Cup teams, in 1978 and 1980. Peter Benka played with conspicuous success in his only Walker Cup, in 1969, but his wife Pam had less success in her two Curtis Cups, in 1966 and 1968. Their son, Mark, was Secretary of Oxford University GC in 1993.

Not all families stick with one sport. Tennis and golf seem to go particularly well together. Catherine Lacoste, the amateur who won the US Ladies' Open in 1967, is the daughter of Simone Thion de la Chaume, winner of

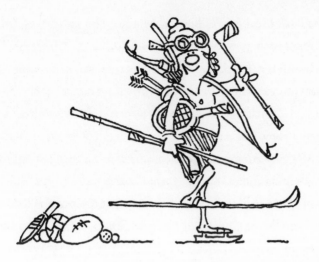

the 1927 Ladies' British Open Amateur Championship, and the great René Lacoste, one of the 'Four Musketeers' of French tennis of the 1920s and 1930s. Lottie Dod, who won Wimbledon in 1887 at the age of 15 and who was never beaten in singles in five years at Wimbledon, played hockey for England at the age of 28, and won the Ladies' British Open Amateur Championship at Troon in 1904, aged 32. She won several skating titles as well, and then completed her international sporting career by winning the silver medal for archery at the 1908 Olympic Games in London. In her spare time, she was an excellent billiards player, and climbed several mountains. In 1935, Alfred Perry won the Open at Muirfield, while at Wimbledon Fred Perry won the men's singles. However, the two Britons were unrelated. The late Ellsworth Vines, the American who won Wimbledon in 1932 and who was the top professional tennis player in the years immediately before the Second World War, became a professional golfer in 1942, and had won five open tournaments by 1945. Mary

Browne of California was an even more remarkable double champion. In 1924, she ranked second in the United States in both tennis and golf, the only person who has achieved such high rankings in the two sports at the same time. She had won three finals (singles, doubles and mixed doubles) on the same day in 1912 at the US Tennis Championships, and 14 years later she won her only Wimbledon title, the women's doubles. In the meantime, in 1924, she lost in the final of the US Ladies' Amateur Championship, having beaten Glenna Collett in the first round. After her retirement from sport, she made a successful career as a portrait painter.

Tennis is not the only other sport at which golfers excel. Sidney Fry, who lost the final of the 1902 Amateur Championship at Hoylake by one hole, was several times British amateur billiards champion. Frank Stranahan, winner of the 1950 Amateur Championship, won the Ohio State Light Heavyweight Weightlifting title in the same year. Chris Hunter, assistant pro at Royal Troon, won the *Daily Express* Cresta Challenge Cup at St Moritz in 1993, taking just 50.66 seconds to complete the run. Mark Roe, winner of the 1992 Trophée Lancôme, was among the top three divers in Britain at junior level, a skill which no doubt stands him in good stead when dealing with water hazards. The incredible Mildred 'Babe' Zaharias played basketball at national level and earned her nickname by hitting five home runs, Babe Ruth style, in a baseball game. She won gold medals as a 19-year-old at the 1932 Olympics, in the 80 metres hurdles (in a world record time of 11.7 seconds), and in the javelin (with a record distance of 43.68 metres).

In the high jump she could only win the silver medal, despite clearing the same height, 1.65 metres, as the winner Jean Shiley. Her Western Roll style was ruled illegal, some say because it was unladylike. Zaharias was not unladylike on the golf course, but she was certainly very powerful. She won seventeen consecutive tournaments in 1946 and 1947, including the Ladies' British Open Amateur title, which she won by 5 and 4 in the final, having lost only four holes in the six rounds of the championship. She won the US Open for the third time in 1954 despite a major operation for cancer the year before. The disease killed her in 1956.

149

Babe Zaharias was too late to have competed in golf at the Olympics, or she would surely have won the title. There have been discussions about bringing golf back as an Olympic sport in time for the Sydney Olympics in the year 2000, which would be 100 years after it was first included. Or not, depending on how you look at it. There was a golf tournament held in Paris in 1900 to coincide with the Olympic Games, but it was not until over eighty years later that Olympic historians confirmed that it had counted as part of the Games. The men's gold medallist was Charles Sands of America, who had been runner-up to Charles Blair MacDonald in the first ever US Amateur Championship in 1895. The women's gold medal was won by Margaret Abbott of Chicago, who was only in Paris to study art, and had no idea she was taking part in the Olympics. She never collected her medal and died in 1955 unaware that she had been the first American woman ever to win an Olympic gold medal. In 1904, in St Louis, the women's event was dropped, but the men's event was far better organized than previously. The winner was George Lyon of Canada, aged 46, who had only taken up golf eight years before, and who beat the US Amateur Champion, H. Chandler Egan, in the final. In 1908, the Olympics were held in Britain and thanks to some internal bickering and inefficiency among the administrators of the event, there was only one entrant – the defending champion George Lyon. He was offered the gold medal by default, but turned it down. Golf has not been an Olympic sport since.

It seems unlikely that golf will be part of the Olympics by the year 2000, at least if an organization calling itself the Global Anti-Golf Movement has its way. The Movement, co-ordinated in Japan – of all unlikely places to find golf haters – sent a letter of protest to the International Olympic Committee saying that 'to make golf an Olympic sport would amount to the IOC endorsing an activity which destroys the environment and brings suffering to local people'. Ah so. From Malaysia came endorsement of this attitude, with a statement from the Asia Pacific People's Environment Network to the effect that golf was the cause of 'severe environmental and social havoc in the Asia Pacific region'.

The severe environmental and social havoc is likely to continue. World No Golf Day, 29 April 1993, was a failure. At least four major professional tournaments started that day in countries as far apart as France and Taiwan, and the attendance on the other 23,996 golf courses estimated to exist around the world was not noticeably lower than usual. Still, among a small and probably not very representative section of the world population, golf is at an end. South Korean politicians have undertaken to give up playing golf, but this is not because of the social or environmental havoc it causes, even when they hack through the rough looking for lost balls. It is because the golf course is where bribes are reputedly most freely given and taken in South Korea, and to play golf is to give the impression of corruption, at least if you are a politician. Golfers and politicians tend to be at opposite ends of the corruptibility spectrum in most parts of the world, but in Korea, the two ends of the spectrum meet under a pot of gold. Allegedly.

151

The cup in the green has become a pot of gold for advertisers in recent seasons. In America, in Japan and soon in all other capitalist golfing nations, you can buy advertising space at the bottom of the cup on each green. As you bend down to pick your ball out of the hole, you will be able to read of the virtues of whatever product is

advertised on a little plastic disc that nestles at the bottom of the cup. This always assumes that most golfers hole out most of the time. Those of us who rely on the generosity of our partners to concede 8-foot putts are unlikely to be much influenced by this subterranean advertising, but at a course in California (where else?) it was shown that golfers' recognition of the beer whose name was at the bottom of the hole rose from zero to 25 per cent after just one round. Whether they went on to buy that beer at the 19th hole is not known.

Stars of other sports have played top-class golf. Nigel Mansell, world champion in two motor racing disciplines, played in the 1992 Australian Open (he missed the cut), and the 1966 Wimbledon champion Manuel Santana became a very fine golfer after giving up professional tennis. Leonard Crawley, who played in four Walker Cup teams, also toured West Indies with the MCC in 1925–26. W.G. Grace, a biography of whom was written by Bernard Darwin, was a keen golfer in his retirement years, having taken up the game when he was past fifty. He was a noisy player, a good driver and a very fine putter, but his iron play was poor. At Walton Heath, he once holed a very long putt which, Darwin said, 'caused him to lie down and roll on the ground in ecstasy'. R.H. de Montmorency, the Eton housemaster who played several international golf matches for Britain between the years 1908 and 1927, when he reached the last eight of the Amateur Championship, was reputed once to have shot 72 at Rye in the morning, and scored 72 for Rye Cricket Club in the afternoon. The embroidered version of the story says that both performances consisted of 18 fours.

Joan Hammond was an Australian youth international golfer. She won the New South Wales LGU title for three years in the 1930s, and was runner-up in the 1933 Australian Ladies' Open. She represented Australia in a match against Great Britain in 1935, and the Australian amateur golf authorities helped raise money for her to study singing in Europe, which she did from 1936. Nigel Kennedy, Kerry Packer and the international bridge player Zia Mahmood are among those who list golf as a recreation in *Who's Who*. So do around 6 per cent of all Members of Parliament (who are less corruptible in Britain than in South Korea), but only four Euro MPs. So does David Spedding, head of MI6, who was obviously brought up on James Bond stories. Ian Fleming's creation played a famous game against Goldfinger, for a shilling a hole, at the fictitious but hardly disguised Royal St Mark's course. Goldfinger cheated wildly, with the aid of his caddie Oddjob, but still lost on the final green.

Caddies have been around since Andrew Dickson was employed to carry the Duke of York's clubs in the 1680s, and Alfie Fyles, who died in 1994, was perhaps the most successful caddie of them all. Like Harry Vardon, he could claim victory in six Opens, as he carried the bags for Gary Player at Carnoustie in 1968, and for Tom Watson in each of his five winning years. Vardon himself began as a caddie in Jersey. He was a gardener to Major Spofforth, the brother of the famous Australian fast bowler, and used to caddie for the Major at the Royal Jersey GC, Grouville. The Major told Vardon, 'Henry, my boy, take my advice

and never give up golf. It may be useful to you some day.'
Incidentally, Abe Mitchell, described by J.H. Taylor as the
finest player who never won an Open, also began his
golfing career as a gardener. He worked for Horace Hutchinson, the Amateur Champion in 1886 and 1887.

It seems unlikely that any other caddie has won as many
Opens as Alfie Fyles, although there have been plenty of
richer ones. Nick Faldo's caddie Fanny Sunesson is
rumoured to make around £250,000 every year, and Lee
Trevino once boasted with some justification that his
caddie ranked among the top twenty money-winners from
his share of his employer's winnings. Not that caddies
have always done so well. Caddies have even gone on
strike from time to time to improve their lot. At Blackpool
in January 1898, they struck for a standard fee of one
shilling a round, up from 9d, as 'the custom of tipping the
caddie has been discontinued'. The golfers of Blackpool
were obviously much meaner than most, as the caddies at
the Wearside Golf Club also struck for the standard rate,

which was then decreed to be 1/6d a round. By 1932, rates had risen, but the striking tendencies of caddies had remained constant. In Westchester County, New York, they struck from 2 to 9 September for the restoration of the $1 fee. They won, despite Henry Kastens' amazing invention of the previous decade. In 1923, he advertised his Henry Kastens Timer: 'Time Your Caddies. Avoid Disputes. Keep An Hour And Minute Record Of Every Caddie. Minutes Mean Money. Lost Time Is Lost Money.' The really odd thing about Mr Kastens' device is that a man as Scrooge-like as he clearly was ever went on to a golf course in the first place, and thus discovered a new problem to challenge his parsimonious mind.

Henry Kastens does not personify the spirit of golf, but perhaps Billy Todd does. Todd was the 24-year-old pro at the County Armagh Golf Club when he flew off to Nairobi to take part in the East African Safari tour in 1981. On arrival at Nairobi Airport, he discovered that his suitcase had gone missing, and in its place had appeared a suitcase full of women's clothes. At least, that was his story and he was sticking to it. Rather than turn up on the tee in drag, Todd sent the suitcase back to England and asked the airline to send on his own case. It never arrived. He was forced to buy a few sets of underwear, trousers and the like, which severely strained his already meagre budget, and though he managed to borrow a few shirts, he complained that it meant doing the washing every day. On the course, life was no more successful than off it. He missed the cut and made no money in the first two events, and then, just as his form was improving in the Zambian Open, he was struck by a stomach bug so virulent that he had to drop out of the tournament and fly home. He made a full recovery, and when he was asked about his African adventures, he could only say, 'I wouldn't have missed it for the world – it's been a great experience.' There speaks a true golfer.

156

DROPPED SHOTS

Ladies-only golf clubs in Britain
Wirral Ladies GC, Birkenhead, founded 1894
Formby Ladies GC, Liverpool, founded 1896
Sunningdale Ladies GC, Surrey, founded 1902

Child named after golf course
Arnaud Massy's daughter named Hoylake, after the scene of his 1907 Open success
James Braid's son named Muirfield, after the scene of his 1901 and 1906 Open successes
Nick Faldo's daughter named Georgia, after the scene of his 1989 and 1990 Masters titles

Withdrawal from tournament after IRA death threats
Neil Coles, Brian Huggett, Bernard Hunt and Peter Oosterhuis among nine golfers who received death threats before Carrolls Irish Open in Dublin, June 1972

Golf by moonlight
Old Prestwick Links, 1864. Old Tom Morris, Dr Knower, Major Crichton and Mr C. Hunter. Began at 11 p.m. in pitch dark, but the moon rose at midnight. Only two balls lost, one each by Dr Knower and Major Crichton in 12 holes played

Golf by headlights
Danny McFie (Royal Mid-Surrey) and George Houghton (Letchworth) in Men's Fourball Bogey final at Letchworth GC, 1949. Last hole, played by lights from cars and a rising moon, was birdied

'*GOLFERS GRUMBLE OVER ECLIPSE*' *of the sun which prevented golf in the afternoon*
Eastern United States, 31 August 1931 (*NY Times* headline)

440 holes played in 12 hours
Robin Jackson, Glenwood GC, Arkansas, 1993

440 holes played in 12 hours
Doug Wert, Coral Springs GC, Florida, 1993

401 holes in 24 hours using only a 6-iron
Ian Colston, Bendigo GC, Victoria, Australia, 27/28 November 1971

376 holes in 24 hours 10 minutes using only a mashie and a putter
Col. W. Farnham, at Guildford Lake GC, Connecticut, 1934

365 holes in 1,403 shots in 39 hours and 49 minutes
DeRoss Kinkade (20), at Hidden Valley GC, from 5.16 a.m. on 29 July 1961

256 holes between dawn and dusk
Charles O'Day (22) at Pleasant View GC, Meriden, Connecticut, 18 July 1932

252 holes in one day
Nick Harley, Simon Gard, Alastair and Patrick Maxwell, Akureyri GC, Iceland, June 1991

Aircraft propeller thrown over clubhouse
when German bomber crashed by first fairway of Royal Wimbledon GC, during Second World War

Troops deployed on golf course
when German troops stationed at the 16th hole at Villa d'Este, Como, Italy, in 1943 to stop passage of Allied POWs escaping from Italian camps

Nazi airmen captured by Open champion
Crew of crashed bomber captured by 1936 champion Alf Padgham, Muswell Hill, Easter Saturday 1943

First man born west of the Mississippi to win an American national championship
George von Elm, US Amateur Champion, 1926

Defending champion forgets to enter tournament
Mark Foster (Worksop), 1992 Carris Trophy winner

Player allowed to compete despite not entering
Laura Davies, Palm Beach Classic at Wycliffe, Lake Worth, Florida, 6 February 1994

Player allowed to compete despite not qualifying, after saving a boy from drowning during qualifying round
Mary Bea Porter, Standard Register Turquoise Classic, Phoenix, Arizona, March 1988

Open Championship lost by camera shutter noise
J.H. Taylor, put off by camera as he drove, 3rd tee, Prestwick, 1914, lost four shots on two holes

Golf clubs in USA when they should have been in South Africa
Tommy Horton's clubs, *en route* from Bermuda to Johannesburg for Horton to defend his South African Open title, 1971

3,147 runs in Test matches, at an average of 101.51, between golf championships
Sir Donald Bradman, Mount Osmond GC, Adelaide, champion in 1935 and 1949

Captain of R&A and President of MCC
H.W. Forster, R&A 1913, MCC 1919
Lord Griffiths, R&A 1993, MCC 1990

Golfing songs
'Straight Down the Middle', recorded by Bing Crosby
'My Miniature Golf Course Min', by Hugh Boswell and Hoyt Brown
'Oh How I Love the Nineteenth Hole When the Eighteenth Hole Is Over', by Frank McIntyre and Percy Wenrich

Golfers who have recorded albums
* Gary Player
Tony Jacklin (with the Mike Sammes Singers)

Golf on the stage
'A Lesson In Golf', a vaudeville act starring Alex J. Morrison and Ed Flanagan, played at Palace Theatre New York for one week from 15 January 1923

Jack Nicklaus's daughter-in-law has appeared as a back-up singer and dancer for Madonna

Golf on the screen

Follow the Sun (1949), Ben Hogan's life story, starring Glenn Ford as Hogan. He was paid $250,000, which was probably more than Hogan made that same year

Golf in literature

The Goff
by Thomas Mathison (1763)

Carminum Rariorum Macaronicorum Delectus (1813)

Golfiana
by George Fullerton Carnegie (1842)

The Expedition of Humphry Clinker
by Tobias Smollett

Round-Up
by Ring Lardner

The Haunted Major
by Robert Marshall

The Sweet Shot
by E.C. Bentley

Goldfinger
by Ian Fleming (1959)

The Heart of a Goof
by P.G. Wodehouse (1926)

Golf in China on China
Plate from collection of Mrs Nellie Ionides, showing 'a group of Occidental-looking men hacking golf balls out of some Oriental-looking sand dunes', sold at Sotheby's in 1964 for £120.

Golf in China
Zheng Wen-jun, first PRC golfer to compete on European Tour, 1994

159